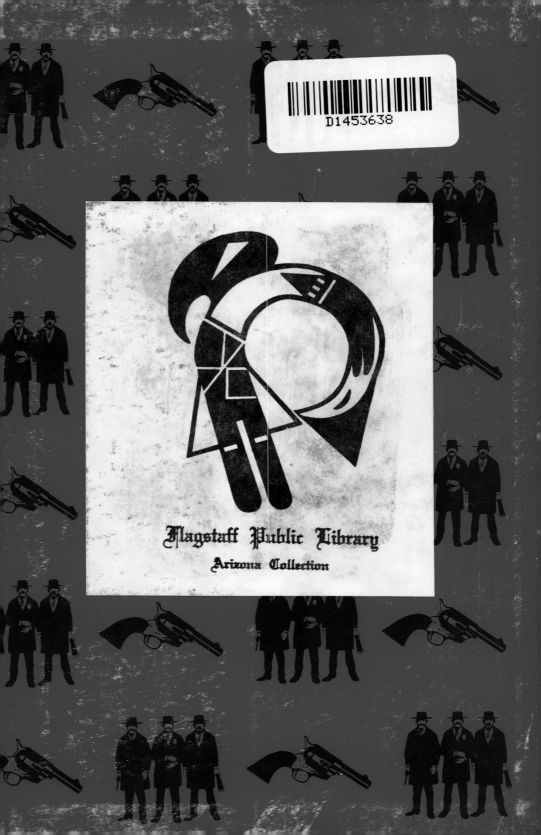

The
EARPS TALK

Edited by Alford E. Turner

HARWOOD HOUSE

EARLE 1980

The EARPS TALK

Edited by Alford E. Turner

Introduction by Glenn G. Boyer
Illustrated by James H. Earle

THE EARLY WEST SERIES
CREATIVE PUBLISHING COMPANY
BOX 9292, PH. 713-846-7907
COLLEGE STATION, TEXAS 77840

THE
EARLY WEST

The Earps Talk

Bibliography: At end of each chapter.
Includes index.
1. Earp, Wyatt Berry Stapp, 1848-1929—Addresses, essays, lectures. 2. Earp, Virgil, d. 1905—Addresses, essays, lectures, 3. Earp, James—Addresses, essays, lectures. 4. Crime and criminals—Southwest, New—History—Addresses, essays, lectures. 5. Frontier and pioneer life—Southwest, New—Addresses, essays, lectures. 6. Southwest, New—History—1848—Addresses, essays, lectures. 7. Peace officers—Southwest, New—Biography—Addresses, essays, lectures.
I. Turner, Alford E. 1912—
F786.E18E185   978'.02'0924   80-11431

ISBN 0-932702-05-8 Regular Edition, 1500 copies
ISBN 0-932702-06-6 Collector's Edition, 25 copies

First Edition, First Printing

i

This book is dedicated
to
Margie Ruth Turner
with gratitude for her unfailing
companionship and love throughout
twenty-two years.

Table of Contents

Glenn G. Boyer is a noted authority on Wyatt Earp who has researched his subject for over thirty years. Most of his writings have been based on primary source materials and interviews with Earp descendants. His most recent book, I MARRIED WYATT EARP, was based on the memoirs of Josephine Sarah Marcus Earp, the wife of Wyatt.

Introduction

This volume by Al Turner is a contribution of *major proportions* to the field of Earpiana. It presents the unabridged words of the Earps that have in the past appeared only in excerpted fashion, usually in footnotes, if at all.

I suspect that the Earp brothers themselves are no more than illusions to most of those who today are fascinated by reading about them. The real Earps, in the hands of gifted writers, have been made bigger than life. Their portraits, in words, are distorted one way or another; as saints or sinners. The land in which they performed the deeds that have made them famous has also been made, in print, a never-never land. Yet it is a very real place. I have lived much of my life in it. It was their size. They were big enough for it. I know it intimately in all its moods. It well could be called Wyatt Earp Country. He is its only native folk hero; it was here that his fame was conceived. That fame burgeoned until, today, he is the only folk hero alive and well anywhere in the English-speaking world.

This book attempts to restore Wyatt Earp to reality in the same sense that his wife's memoirs attempted that. Wyatt himself had no idea he was destined to be a folk hero. Probably if he had been given a choice in the matter, being a gambler, he would have flipped a coin on it. But he likely would not have given a damn which way the coin came down.

When he was young he undoubtedly was a showman. But so were his contemporaries in his business. It was a helpful adjunct of survival in his trade as a lawman. If the bad ones thought that you had knocked over a couple of dozen of their kind before them, it naturally shook them. They were easier to handle as a result. Wild Bill practiced this excusable deception. Bat Masterson probably did so with a greater degree of success than anyone. Writers who should have discovered better are still stung by the Masterson propoganda fallout, repeating tales about the 26 men he had killed, for example. (He had to steal two from his brother, Ed, to get his score up to three.)

The stories in this book from the San Francisco *Examiner* reveal Wyatt Earp as practicing that "exaggerating" part of the trade, in my opinion. Further, and it is a fact that seems to have escaped nearly everyone, these stories appeared just when it was reasonably expected that a Republican administration might assume office in Washington. Wyatt Earp was growing older, was bored with the sporting business he was soon to quit, and probably was missing the exhiliration of the old man-hunting days. It is reasonable to assume that his friends, the Hearsts, backed his bid to become U.S. Marshal of Arizona under McKinley. It is a moot question how far the deal went. It is a fact that Mrs. Earp, fearful of Wyatt's old enemies in Arizona, scotched the thing in the end. Her husband put a good face on it by saying that he declined the job. In the first place, however, these *Examiner* articles furthered his chances of being offered the job. How much of the articles he himself actually provided is another moot question. My guess would be that he gave merely the outlines. An imaginative Hearst literary hack probably fleshed them out. Wyatt, we may safely guess, was uninterested in the details. This is only my supposition. Nonetheless these articles contained many factual insights into his life.

The interviews with Wyatt's older brothers, James and Virgil, took place under less contrived circumstances. They are news interviews where the speaker had no particular axe to grind. They are, on the whole, more acceptable as unvarnished fact, due to that circumstance.

To many readers, Al Turner will need no introduction. For those others, let me say that I consider him the foremost authority on the Earp Saga. He has devoted a substantial portion of his almost seventy years to collecting everything he could uncover regarding the Earps. His home is one vast library of old and new books, ancient newspaper clippings, copies of official documents from the crumbling files of bygone years, letters, photographs— many of them of Earps who are, if known at all, usually only names in the Earp Saga—taped interviews with those who knew the Earp Brothers and a literal bonanza of allied material. His mind is a file of names, events and conclusions about the Earps, based on a store of information almost as detailed as though he had lived their adventures with them.

Further, and perhaps most importantly, Turner is generously willing to share his expertise, whether with those seriously interested in the Earps as they really were, or with those interested only in the myth that has grown up around them. He has not fallen victim to that strange *secrecy-syndrome* that infects so many researches in this genuinely "fey" area of Western history. This is certainly evidenced by the fact that he publishes.

Finally, I must comment on the weird circumstances that vast hordes of people seem to have found life more endurable from vicariously sharing the story-book mastery of a hostile environment (as Stuart Lake noted) through the fictional adventures of a phanton, known as Wyatt Earp. I do not maliciously intrude upon the happy illusions of this group, but feel they are worthy of note. As a factual writer in the Earp field, I have felt this cult's wrath whenever I refused to become fossilized in a permanent niche that pleased them—or did not seem to reverence their unfounded beliefs. I sense that, with the publication of this major book in this field, Turner is about to share my fate as a writer.

I feel that Al will be adequately compensated by the knowledge that he has advanced the business of restoring the never-never Earps to some semblance of humanity, and hence reality.

Al and I both live down here in Wyatt Earp Country, where the real man's achievements seem a great deal easier to grasp. We can walk into the Chochise County Courthouse at Bisbee any day and find a hundred original Wyatt Earp signatures* on documents attesting to what he really did. This is the country where he fought the bitter bloody battles that eventually made him a folk hero. It is also the country where the proof yet resides to show that he did both more and less than has been claimed for him by opposing chroniclers. It's a lot easier to get him in true focus on this, his home turf. The reader should never lose sight of the fact that Turner, in annotating this work, had access to this vast reservoir of primary source material.

The verdict if one is needed is this—Wyatt Earp was a helluva good man to have around—provided you were not a crook or a phoney. The same can be said for his brothers, Jim, Virge, and Morgan. They were known as the Fighting Earps and the title fit them well. Most of us would have liked them. If the reader does not find Turner's Wyatt Earp to his liking, it will not be because the portrait is not accurate. It may be because the reader is disappointed by not again meeting that *Phantom*—the Wyatt Earp that exists only in his own glowing imagination, a creation that soothes some inner need that reality cannot touch.

Glenn G. Boyer
Bisbee, Arizona
February 1980

*To say nothing of those of his better known cohorts such as Doc Holliday, the other Earp Brothers, Kate Elder and many lesser known ones, who nonetheless were part of the myth-making process, such as Andy Neff, or Oregin Charles Smith (known as Hairlip Charlie) and a host of others.

Alford E. Turner of Tombstone, Arizona, is recognized by many as the leading authority on Earpiana, having researched and studied their deeds and involvements for thirty years. Mr. Turner has annotated this book with primary research that was taken from the official records as they exist today.

Author's Preface

From out of the turbulence and gun smoke that swirled about the streets of early Tombstone, the Earp brothers and their cohort, Doc Holliday, stand out boldly in the tales that describe that wild town. They are remembered either as exponents of law and order, or clever desperadoes hiding behind their badges— depending on whose story you choose to believe.

Both of these versions of the Earp story are partisan in nature, being based either on an embellishment, or distortion of the facts. A number of popular authors laid the foundation for the pro-Earp version of the story; but most of these versions were not completely supported by facts. Among these were: Alfred Henry Lewis, *The Sunset Trail*, 1905; William Barclay (Bat) Masterson, *Famous Gunfighters of the Western Frontier*, 1907; Frederick R. Bechdolt, *When the West Was Young*, 1922; Walter Noble Burns, *Tombstone: An Iliad of the Southwest*, 1927; and Stuart N. Lake, *Wyatt Earp: Frontier Marshal*, 1931. All of these authors described the Earps in the heroic mold.

Although these writings gave the Earp brothers a lasting place in the folklore of the American West, they also created the Earp "Achilles heel" to be counterattacked. A second group of writers centered their assult upon the "strawman of fiction" that the pro-Earp writers had created. They found nothing good to say about the Earps and Doc Holliday. The first of these was William M. Breakenridge in his book, *Helldorado*, 1928. He had been a part-time deputy sheriff in Cochise County, but his principal occupations had been that of jail guard, jail janitor, process server, and census tabulator. His dislike for the Earps and Holliday ran deep, perhaps because of envy.

Other writers who wrote in a manner that was negative to the Earp image followed: Frank Waters, *The Earp Brothers of Tombstone*, 1960; Ed Bartholomew, *Wyatt Earp: The Untold Story*, 1963, and *Wyatt Earp: The Man and the Myth*, 1964; Ramon F. Adams, *Burs Under the Saddle*, 1964; and Odie B. Faulk, *Tombstone: Myth and Reality*, 1972.

Reading the two groups of books listed above clearly reveals the extremes of partisanship that has resulted in a dual evaluation of the character of Wyatt Earp. In the first listing he is presented as a crusading disposer of badmen, a knight without fault; and in the second, as Frank Waters says, "an itinerant saloon keeper, cardsharp, gunman, bigamist, church deacon, policeman, bunko artist, and supreme confidence man." Neither position is correct. A true evaluation of his character would fall somewhere between these extremes.

In spite of numerous contradictions found in the works of the debunkers, their versions usually started with the retaliatory testimony given by Ike Clanton at the Spicer Hearing that followed the "O.K. Corral Fight." His garbled testimony about an Earp gang of stage robbers who "piped off" money from Wells Fargo and covered up their crimes by robbery and murder, was devised to save Clanton's hide from his own gang.

As it was, Wyatt wanted to be sheriff of Cochise County and believed that the "glory" of capturing the Benson stage robbers, Leonard, Head, and Crane, would help him at the polls. He offered the express company's reward of $1,200 each for the capture of the highwaymen to Ike Clanton, Tom and Frank McLaury, and Joe Hill. Their job was to lure the bandits to the McLaury Ranch where Earp could capture them. The plot fell through, however, when Joe Hill, the contact man, rode to the Clanton Ranch in the Animas Valley of New Mexico and learned that Leonard and Head had been killed in another difficulty. Crane was also killed a short time later while driving cattle in Skelton Canyon with Old Man Clanton. The Judas Iscariot "give away" of the highwaymen failed; Earp received no "glory" and the Clantons and McLaurys no money. Ike Clanton's testimony remained, however, forming the foundation for those who wished to discredit Wyatt Earp.

Another source used by the bebunking writers were the stories about the Earps handed down by ranchers to their children and friends by word of mouth. It was easy for cattlemen to like the "cowboys" because of a similar life style; they wore the same type of clothing, lived isolated lives in lonely places, worked from sunrise to sunset, and made their living by raising stock. The Earps, on the other hand, were an enigma to the ranchers. They were city dudes, wore fancy clothes, bathed several times times a week, and made their living by gambling and police work. The mere fact that they were law enforcement officers at various times caused many ranchers to dislike them. Numerous early day cattlemen were rustlers themselves; others worked for the rustlers and took their wages in stolen cattle. It can be said for the ranchers, however, that when their various ranges were stocked, they became "honest;" but unjust hatred for the Earps remained and the ranchers lost no opportunity to criticize them. Seldom is it possible to find a rancher who has anything but contempt for the work of the Earps, and this attitude found its way into the literature of the Southwest.

Another source of anti-Earp material was produced by historians of the region. Substituting interviews with partisan old-timers for primary research, they did little but perpetrate fiction.

James H. McClintock, Arizona's State Historian, was the first professional to denounce the Earps in his three-volume work, *Arizona, the Youngest State*, 1916. Following the lead of Ike Clanton, McClintock said the following about the Earps:

"All the Earps were professional gamblers. They were charged, first and last, with almost half of the robberies that were of such frequent occurrence on the roads leading out of the camp."

In spite of Mr. McClintock's assertion, the Earps were never charged in any court with stage robbery, and the only explicit charge made by an individual against them was that made by Ike Clanton at the Spicer Hearing. Ike was seeking revenge for the death of his younger brother, and attempting to save himself from the wrath of his gang.

Mr. McClintock's anti-Earp attitude can be attributed to the fact that he personally knew a number of Tombstone old-timers, including William M. Breakenridge, whom he had accompanied on a survey trip through Maricopa County in 1889. Undoubtedly Billy, Wyatt's enemy, told the future State Historian the tales that both men later used in their books.

Another debunker of the Earps, Frank C. Lockwood, a literature professor at the University of Arizona, described Wyatt Earp as a professional gunfighter and a cold-blooded killer in his book, *Pioneer Days in Arizona*, 1932. Earp was neither. Although handy with a gun, Wyatt Earp engaged in only one stand-up gunfight on a man-to-man basis. This was his shotgun duel with Curly Bill Brocius at Mescal Springs (Iron Springs) in which the cowboy leader was killed. As a member of posses, he participated in the killing of a number of other men including George Hoyt, Billy Clanton, Frank Stilwell, Florentino, Johnny Barnes, and Johnny Ringo.

Since Wyatt Earp was a businessman, whose purpose was to earn money, it is difficult to understand why most of the writing about him centers on his law enforcement work, an occupation that consumed less than five years of his life. The real man was engaged in numerous occupations, among which were: express company detective, prospector, mine operator, oil well speculator, real estate salesman, racehorse handler, prize fight referee, saloon owner and gambler.

The last historian to be discussed is Ramon F. Adams, the Dallas businessman, collector, lexicographer, and bibliophile, considered by many to be the foremost authority on Western outlaws and gunfighters. Mr. Adams has made significant contributions to Western history with his books, but his writings about the Earps contain many errors.

A great deal of Mr. Adams' evaluation of the Earps came from secondary sources. He reviewed many books that were written by uninformed or prejudiced authors. He lists 184 citations referring to the Earps and Holliday in *Burs Under the Saddle*, and many of them contain errors.

Much of the confusion that Mr. Adams experienced when reviewing the writings about the Earps was brought about by the fact that he accepted Lake's book, *Wyatt Earp: Frontier Marshal*, as being Earp's authentic biography. He assumed that Stuart N. Lake recorded the incidents and conversations that Earp had related to him. This was not true because Lake did not know the whole story, and fictionalized parts of the book. Consequently, Ramon Adams' attack was on the "strawman of fiction" created by Stuart Lake, not the real Wyatt Earp.

The interviews and testimonies that appear in this book do not depend upon the partisan writings of either the legend makers or the debunkers. They were told by the Earp brothers themselves, Wyatt, Virgil, and James, who lived the actions that are described. Most of these accounts were reported contemporary with the incidents that they describe, with the exception of the three interviews given by Wyatt Earp to the San Francisco *Examiner* in 1896. Wyatt was a relatively young man of 48 years when he related these stories, and his memory should have been clear in recalling these major incidents of his life.

There are two possible sources of errors in these interviews. First, a large number of old-timers gave themselves benefit of the doubt when recounting their experiences; secondly, the very nature of the twice-told interview process of reporting was error-prone. The storyteller was not always quoted correctly by the interviewer. In this book, most mistakes have been eliminated from their work by comparing the original stories with known facts taken from primary research, and pointing out apparent errors in the notes that follow each chapter.

Wyatt Earp continues to be a misunderstood man, and probably will remain so to many people. He was more of a businessman than a lawman and gunfighter, yet most reporting about him concerns violence.

Glenn G. Boyer sized the situation up quite accurately in his "Postscripts to Historical Fiction About Wyatt Earp in Tombstone," *Arizona and the West*, Autumn, 1976, with the following paragraph:

"The writers who have sought to judge and convict the Earps probably never suspected (nor would have cared had they known) that diligent research would reveal a different portrait of the Earps. This is due in part to the strange curse that clouds all study of the clan. Reacting with typical ambivalence toward Wyatt Earp, who in life made lasting friends or bitter enemies, writers have either praised or derided him. There is no middle ground. Logic, reason and facts make little impression. Yet Wyatt has somehow become a genuine folk hero, a posthumous fate which probably would have quietly pleased him as being a final triumph over spiteful enemies. He would have recognized that he did not deserve the elevation. But neither has he earned the derogatory historical fiction that has been repeated about him."

Alford E. Turner
Tombstone, Arizona
February 1980

xvii   The Earps Talk

Acknowledgements

I am deeply indebted to the following people who provided me with the assistance and encouragement necessary for the completion of this book: Glenn G. Boyer, who freely gave access to his unique Cason and Colyn Collections, including interviews with numerous Earp family members; Carl Chafin—for his expertise in the history of the development of the town of Tombstone, Arizona; Robert Palmquist—lawyer, Western buff extraordinary, and friend; and Jim Earle—historian, collector, and publisher, for his patience and generous help in bringing this work to press.

I am grateful to William Oster—educator and researcher, in remembrance of many happy hours and days while we patiently put our tracks down on the trail of the Earps and their fascinating coterie of followers; Fred Holladay—for the use of his excellent history of the Earp clan in San Bernardino County, California; David H. Cruickshanks—for the use of his definitive genealogy of the Earp family in England; and Don Shumar—historian and weapons expert for his assistance and advice.

Special thanks go to Christine Rhodes, Cochise County Recorder, and her deputies Larry Elkins, and Vi Chizewsky, who made the county records an open book for me; Marguerite B. Cooley—Director of the Department of Library and Archives at the State Capitol in Phoenix, Arizona; and Sidney B. Brinckerhoff—Director of the Arizona Historical Society in Tucson.

The
EARPS TALK

Chapter 1

WYATT TALKS

The following interview with Wyatt Earp appeared in THE EXAMINER, a San Francisco newspaper, on Sunday morning, August 2, 1896. The article was entitled, "How Wyatt Earp Routed a Gang of Arizona Outlaws."

It may be that the trail of blood will seem to lie too thickly over the pages that I write.[1] If I had it in me to invent a tale, I would fain lighten the crimson stain so that it would glow no deeper than a demure pink. But half a lifetime on the frontier attunes a man's hand to the six-shooter rather than to the pen, and it is lucky that I am asked for facts, for more than facts I could not give.

Half a lifetime of such turbulent days and nights as will never again be seen in this, or, I believe, in any land, might be expected to tangle a man's brain with memories none to easy to sift apart. But for the cornerstone of this episodic narrative, I cannot make a better choice than the bloody feud in Tombstone, Arizona,[2] which cost me a brave brother and cost more than one worthless life among the murderous dogs who pursued me and mine only less bitterly than I pursued them.

And so I marshal my characters. My stalwart brothers, Virgil, Morgan, shall stand on the right of the stage with my dear old comrade, Doc Holliday; on the left shall be arrayed Ike Clanton, Sheriff Behan, Curly Bill, and the rest. Fill in the stage with miners, gamblers, rustlers, stage robbers, murderers and cowboys, and the melodrama is ready to begin. Nor shall a heroine be wanting, for Big Nose Kate[3] was shaped for the part by nature and circumstances. Poor Kate! Frontier whiskey must have laid her low long since. And that gives me an opportunity to introduce the reader to both Doc Holliday and Kate by telling of an episode in their checkered lives two years before the action of my melodrama begins.

Big Nose Kate [Kate Fisher], Doc Holliday's woman, as she appeared in 1890.

It happened in 1877, when I was City Marshal of Dodge City, Kansas.[4] I had followed the trail of some cattle thieves across the border into Texas,[5] and during a short stay in Fort Griffin, I first met Doc Holliday and the woman who was known variously as Big Nose Kate, Kate Fisher, and, on occasions of ceremony, Mrs. Doc Holliday. Holliday asked me a good many questions about Dodge City and seemed inclined to go there, but before he had made up his mind about it, my business called me over to Fort Clark. It was while I was on my way back to Fort Griffin that my new friend and his Kate found it necessary to pull their stakes hurriedly. Whereof the plain, unvarnished facts were these:[6]

Doc Holliday was spending the evening in a poker game, which was his custom whenever faro bank did not present superior claims on his attention. On his right sat Ed Bailey, who needs no description because he is soon to drop out of this narrative. The trouble began, as it was related to me afterward, by Ed Bailey monkeying with the deadwood, or what people who live in cities call discards. Doc Holliday admonished him once or twice to "play poker"—which is your seasoned gambler's method of

Wyatt S. Earp in 1887 at about the time that he moved to San Diego and tried the real estate business.

cautioning a friend to stop cheating—but the misguided Bailey persisted in his furtive attentions to the deadwood. Finally, having detected him again, Holliday pulled down a pot without showing his hand, which he had a perfect right to do. Thereupon Bailey started to throw his gun around on Holliday, as might have been expected. But before he could pull the trigger, Doc Holliday had jerked a knife out of his breast-pocket and with one sideways sweep had caught Bailey just below the brisket.

Well, that broke up the game, and pretty soon Doc Holliday was sitting cheerfully in the front room of the hotel, guarded while the gamblers clamored for his blood. You see, he had not lived in Fort Griffin very long, while Ed Bailey was well liked. It wasn't long before Big Nose Kate, who had a room downtown, heard about the trouble and went up to take a look at her Doc through a back window. What she saw and heard led her to think that his life wasn't worth ten minutes purchase, and I don't believe it was. There was a shed at the back of the lot, and a horse was stabled in it. She was a kindhearted girl was Kate, for she went to the trouble of leading the horse into the alley and tethering it there before she set fire to the shed. She also got a six-

Kate Elder [Kate Fisher] lived and worked at the Cochise Hotel in Cochise, Arizona, from 1899-1900. (Turner Collection)

shooter from a friend down the street, which, with the one she always carried, made two.

It all happened just as she had planned it. The shed blazed up and she hammered at the door, yelling, "Fire!" Everybody rushed out, except the Marshal, and the constables and their prisoner. Kate walked in as bold as a lion, threw one of her six-shooters on the Marshal and handed the other to Doc Holliday.

"Come on, Doc," she said with a laugh.

He didn't need any second invitation and the two of them backed out of the hotel, keeping the officers covered. All that night they hid among the willows down by the creek, and early next morning a friend of Kate's brought them two horses and some of Doc Holliday's clothes from his room. Kate dressed up in a pair of pants, a pair of boots, a shirt and a hat, and the pair of them got away safely and rode the four hundred miles to Dodge City, where they were installed in great style when I got back home.

Which reminds me that during my absence the man whom I had left behind as a deputy had been killed by some cowboys who were engaged in the fascinating recreation known as "shootin' up the town."[7] This incident is merely mentioned as a further sign of the time, and a further excuse for the blood which cannot but trickle through the web of my remembrance.

Such, then, was the beginning of my acquaintance with Doc Holliday, the mad, merry scamp with heart of gold and nerves of steel; who, in the dark years that followed stood at my elbow in many a battle to the death. He was a dentist, but he preferred to be a gambler. He was a Virginian, but he preferred to be a frontiersman and a vagabond. He was a philosopher, but he preferred to be a wag. He was long, lean, an ash-blond and the quickest man with a six-shooter I ever knew.[8] It wasn't long after I returned to Dodge City that his quickness saved my life. He saw a man draw on me behind my back. "Look out, Wyatt!" he shouted, but while the words were coming out his mouth he had jerked his pistol out of his pocket and shot the other fellow before the latter could fire.[9]

On such incidents as that are built the friendships of the frontier.

In 1879 Dodge City was beginning to lose much of the snap which had given it a charm to men of restless blood, and I decided to move to Tombstone, which was just building up a reputation. Doc Holliday thought he would move with me. Big Nose Kate had left him long before—they were always a quarrelsome couple—and settled in Las Vegas, New Mexico. He looked her up en route, and, the old tenderness reasserted itself; she resolved to throw in her lot with his in Arizona.[10] As for me, I was tired of the trials of a peace officer's life and wanted no more of it. But as luck would have it, I stopped at Prescott, Arizona, to see my brother Virgil and while there I met C. P. Dake, the United States Marshal of the Territory. Dake had heard of me before, and he begged me so hard to take the deputyship in Tombstone that I finally consented. It was thus that the real troubles of a lifetime began.[11]

The boom had not struck Tombstone then, but it did a few months later, when the mills for treating the ore were completed and tales about the fabulous richness of the silver mines were bruited abroad. Before long the town had a population of ten to twelve thousand, of whom about three hundred were cattle thieves, stage robbers, murderers, and outlaws.

For the first eight months I worked as a shotgun messenger for Wells, Fargo & Company and beyond the occasional excitement of an abortive holdup and a few excursions after cattle thieves and homicides in my official capacity, everything was quiet as a grave. Then the proprietors of "The Oriental," the biggest gambling house in town, offered to take me in partnership. [12] One of them—his name was Rickabaugh and he was a San Francisco man—was unpopular, and a coterie of the tough gamblers was trying to run the firm out of town.

The proprietors of the Oriental had an idea that their troubles would cease if they had the Deputy United States Marshal for a partner, and so it proved, for a time at least. So I turned over my position with Wells, Fargo & Company to my brother Morgan, who held it for six months, after which I gave him a job in "The Oriental." My brother Virgil had also joined me, and when the town was incorporated, he was appointed Chief of Police. [13]

About this time was laid the foundation of the vendetta which became the talk of the frontier and resulted in no end of bloodshed.

A band of rustlers held up the coach and killed the driver and one of the passengers. Virgil and I, with another man, followed them into the mountains for seventeen days, but our horses gave out and they got away from us. When we got back to town I went to Ike Clanton, who was sort of a leader among the rustlers, and offered to give him all the $6,000 reward offered by Wells, Fargo & Company if he would lead me to where I could arrest the murderers. After thinking about it deeply he agreed to send a partner of his, named Joe Hill, to lead them from where they were hiding to some place within twenty-five miles of Tombstone, where I could get them. But in case I killed his partner he wanted to be sure that the reward would be paid alive or dead. In order to assure him, I got Wells, Fargo's agent, Marshall Williams, to telegraph to San Francisco about it, and a reply came in the affirmative.

So Clanton sent Hill off to decoy the men I wanted. That was to take several days, and in the meantime Marshall Williams got drunk, and, suspecting that I was using Ike Clanton for some purpose, tried to pump him about it. Clanton was terrified at the thought of any third person knowing of our bargain and accused me of having told Doc Holliday. Fear and whiskey robbed Clanton of his discretion and he let out his secret to Holliday, who had known nothing about it. Doc Holliday, who was the soul of honor, berated him vigorously for his treachery, and the conversation was heard by several people.

That was enough for Clanton. He knew that his only alternative was to kill us or be killed by his own people. Early next morning Virgil and I were told that he was out with a Winchester and a six-shooter looking for us. So we went out looking for him, taking different routes. Virgil was going down Fourth Street when Clanton came out of a hallway, looking in the opposite direction. "I want you, Ike," said Virgil, walking up behind him. Clanton threw his gun around and tried to take a shot, but Virgil knocked it away, pulled his own and arrested his man. Ike was fined $25 for disturbing the peace.[14] Ike Clanton's next move was to telegraph to Charleston, ten miles away, for Billy Clanton, Tom McLowery, Frank McLowery, and Bill Clayton [sic] hard men, every one. They came galloping into town, loaded up with ammunition and swearing to kill us off in short order.[15] Thirty or forty citizens offered us their help, but we said we could manage the job alone. "What had we better do?" asked Virgil. "Go arrest 'em," said I.

The four newcomers and Ike Clanton stationed themselves on a fifteen foot lot between two buildings across the street and sent us word that if we did not come down there and fight they would waylay and kill us.[16] So we started down after them—Doc Holliday, Virgil, Morgan, and I. As we came to the lot they moved back and backs against one of the buildings.

"I'm going to arrest you, boys," said Virgil.

For answer, their six-shooters began to spit. Frank McLowery fired at me and Billy Clanton at Morgan. Both missed. I had a gun in my overcoat pocket and I jerked it out at Frank McLowery hitting him in the stomach. At the same time Morgan shot Billy Clanton in the breast. So far we had got the best of it, but just then Tom McLowery, who got behind his horse, fired under the animal's neck and bored a hole right through Morgan sideways. The bullet entered one shoulder and came out at the other.

"I've got it, Wyatt!" said Morgan.

HARWOOD HOUSE

"Then get behind me and keep quiet," I said—but he didn't.

By this time bullets were flying so fast that I could not keep track of them. Frank McLowery had given a yell when I shot him, and made for the street, with his hand over his stomach. Ike Clanton and Billy Clanton were shooting fast, and so was Virgil, and the two latter made a break for the street. I fired a shot which hit Tom McLowery's horse and made it break away, and Doc Holliday took the opportunity to pump a charge of buckshot out of a Wells Fargo shotgun into Tom McLowery, who promptly fell dead. In the excitement of the moment, Doc Holliday didn't know what he had done and flung away the shotgun in disgust, pulling his six-shooter instead.

Then I witnessed a strange spectacle. Frank McLowery and Billy Clanton were sitting in the middle of the street, both badly wounded, but emptying their six-shooters like lightning. One of them shot Virgil through the leg, and he shot Billy Clanton. Then Frank McLowery started to his feet and staggered across the street, though he was full of bullets. On the way he came face to face with Doc Holliday.

"I've got ye now, Doc," he said.

"Well, you're a good one if you have," said Holliday with a laugh.

With that they both aimed. But before you can understand what happened next, I must carry the narrative back half a minute:

After the first exchange in the lot, Ike Clanton had got into one of the buildings from the rear and when I reached the street he was shooting out of one of the front wndows. Seeing him aim at Morgan, I shouted: "Look out, Morg, you're getting it in the back!"

Morgan wheeled around and in doing so fell on his side. While in that position he caught sight of Doc Holliday and Frank McLowery aiming at each other. With a quick drop he shot McLowery in the head. At the same instant, McLowery's pistol flashed and Doc Holliday was shot in the hip.

That ended the fight. Ike Clanton and Billy Clayton [*sic*] ran off and made haste to give themselves up to the sheriff, for the citizens were out a hundred strong to back us up.

I have described this battle with as much particularity as possible, partly because there are not many city dwellers who have more than a vague idea of what such a fight really means, and partly because I was rather curious to see how it would look in cold type. It may or may not surprise some readers to learn that from the first to the last shot fired, not more than a minute elapsed. [17]

Of the exciting events which followed, I can give no more than a brief account. The principal factor in all that happened was Sheriff Johnny Behan, my political rival and personal enemy. Doc Holliday and I were arrested on a charge of murder. My two brothers were exempt from his proceeding because they were both disabled. We were acquitted at the preliminary hearing and rearrested on another warrant charging the same offense.

WELLS FARGO SHOTGUN
USED BY
WYATT EARP
AT IRON SPRINGS ARIZON A MARCH 1882
STEVENS 10 GAUGE SHOTGUN #927

Fred J. Dodge wrote to Stuart Lake on October 12, 1931, and stated that this Wells Fargo shotgun was used by Wyatt to kill Curly Bill on March 24, 1882. It had been loaned to Wyatt by Dodge who was an undercover agent for Wells Fargo & Co. at the time. (Earle Collection)

This time the hearing was held at Contention, nine miles from Tombstone, and we would have been assassinated on the road had not a posse of the best citizens insisted on accompanying the Sheriff as a guard. The hearing was never completed, because Holliday and I were released on a writ of *habeas corpus.* In the meantime, the Grand Jury persistently refused to indict us.[18]

But the determination to assassinate us never relaxed. Three months later, Virgil was returning home to the hotel, and when he was halfway across the street five double-barreled shotguns were discharged at him from an ambuscade. One shot shattered his left arm and another passed through his body. I arrested several of the assassins, but twenty or thirty rustlers swore to an alibi and they were acquited.[19]

Three months later, before Virgil had recovered from his wounds, Morgan was shot dead through the glass door of a saloon, while he was playing a game of pool. I sent his body home to Colton, California, and shipped off Virgil—a physical wreck—on the same train from Tucson. But even at the depot I was forced to fight Ike Clanton and four or five of his friends who had followed us to do murder. One of them, named Frank Stilwell, who was believed to be Morgan's murderer, was killed by my gun going off when he grasped it.[20] When I returned to Tombstone, Sheriff Behan came to arrest me, but I refused to surrender and he weakened.

For a long time thereafter I occupied the anomalous position of being a fugitive from the county authorities, and performing the duties of Deputy United States Marshal, with the sanction and moral support of my chief.

With Doc Holliday and one or two faithful comrades, I went into camp among the hills and withstood more than one attack from outlaws who had been implicated in the death of one brother and the disablement of another—attacks which resulted fatally to some of my enemies and left me without a scratch.

One such encounter I will describe because it illustrates as well as anything what could come of the exigencies of a frontier vendetta.

We had ridden twenty-five miles over the mountains with the intention of camping at a certain spring. As we got near the place I had a presentiment that something was wrong, and unlimbered my shotgun. Sure enough, nine cowboys sprang from the bank where the spring was and began firing at us. I jumped off my horse to return the fire, thinking my men would do the same, but they retreated.

One of the cowboys, who was trying to pump some lead into me with a Winchester, was a fellow named Curly Bill, a stage robber whom I had been after for eight months, and for whom I had a warrant in my pocket.

I fired both barrels of my gun into him, blowing him all to pieces.

With that the others jumped into a clump of willows and kept on firing, so I retreated, keeping behind my horse. He was a high-strung beast, and the firing frightened him so that whenever I tried to get my Winchester from the saddle he would rear up and keep it out of my reach. When I had backed out about a hundred yards, I started to mount. Now, it was a hot day, and I had loosened my cartridge belt two or three holes. When I tried to get astride, I found that it had fallen down over my thighs, keeping my legs together. While I was perched up thus, trying to pull my belt higher with one hand, the horn of the saddle was shot off. However, I got away all right, and just then my men rallied. But I did not care to go back at the rustlers, so we sought out another water hole for camp. The skirt of my overcoat was shot to pieces on both sides, but not a bullet touched me. [21]

The shotgunning of Curly Bill

JIM
EARLE
NOV 73

Sheriff Behan trailed us with a big posse composed of rustlers, but it was only a bluff, for when I left word for him where he could find us and waited for him to come, he failed to appear.[22]

My best friends advised me to leave the Territory, so I crossed into Colorado. While I was there, they tried to get a requisition for me, but the Governor refused to sign it.[23]

It's an old story now. I have been in Arizona in recent years—as near Tombstone as Tucson, in fact—but no one sought to molest me. The outlaws who were my worst enemies are mostly killed off or in the penitentiary. Poor Doc Holliday died of consumption three years ago in Colorado.[24] My brother Virgil is running a stock ranch in Texas. A large section of his upper arm is entirely without bone, and yet he can use his fingers.

On reading it over it seems to me that there is not only too much blood, but too much of myself in my story. However, a man gets in the habit of thinking about himself when he spends half a lifetime on the frontier.

Wyatt S. Earp

HISTORICAL NOTES AND EDITORIAL COMMENTS

1. The vocabulary and composition of this article is obviously the work of a professional writer—not that of an unschooled frontiersman such as Wyatt Earp. Earp gave the story to a San Francisco *Examiner* reporter in interview form, with the newsman recording the article later from notes. The fact that Wyatt Earp was the narrator cannot be doubted, however, because his expressions appear time and again throughout the article, for example: "to pull up their stakes," "monkeying with the deadwood," "throw his gun on Holliday," "jerked a knife," "threw one of his six-shooters on the marshal," and, "I had a gun in my overcoat pocket and I jerked it out at Frank McLowery [sic]."

2. Earp was referring to the Earp-Clanton feud; perhaps more justifiably called the Cochise County War, or the Earp-Behan feud. In any case, the vendetta started with the so called "O.K. Corral" gunfight in which three men were killed, the McLaury brothers and Billy Clanton; and two Earps were wounded, Virgil and Morgan. This sanguine encounter between "cowboys" and lawmen on October 26, 1881, was the beginning of a war that ended nineteen years later with the killing of Warren Earp in Wilcox, Arizona, in 1900.

A letter from Will McLaury to his father dated April 13, 1884, (Arizona Historical Society) states that he sought the services of assassins to revenge the death of his two younger brothers. He hired a number of "cowboys," including such men as Pete Spence, Florentino, Hank Swilling, "John Doe" Freis, and Indian Charley, to kill the Earp brothers and a number of their allies. The "contract men" managed to assassinate Morgan Earp and wound Virgil; but failed in their attempt to kill Judge Spicer, Marshall Williams, Thomas Fitch, John P. Clum, Wyatt Earp, and Doc Holiday.

PARTICIPANTS OF THE "O. K. CORRAL" FIGHT

"Cowboys"

Joseph Isaac Clanton
Robert Finley (Frank) McLaury
Thomas Clark McLaury
William C. Claiborne
Wesley Fuller
William Clanton

Earps [Lawmen]

Wyatt Stapp Earp
Virgil Walter Earp
Morgan S. Earp
John H. (Doc) Holliday

PERSONS KILLED IN THE FEUD

"Cowboys"

William Clanton, October 26, 1881
Robert Finley (Frank) McLaury, October 26, 1881
Thomas Clark McLaury, October 26, 1881
Frank Stilwell, March 20, 1882
Florentino, March 22, 1882
William (Curly Bill) Brocius, March 24, 1882
Johnny Barnes, died of wounds received, March 24, 1882
John Peter Ringo, about July 10-12, 1882.

Earps [Lawmen]

Morgan S. Earp, March 18, 1882
Warren Baxter Earp, July 6, 1900

VARIOUS BATTLES OF THE FEUD

Engagement	Date	Location	Results
"O. K. Corral" Fight	Oct. 26, 1881	Fremont & Third Streets, Tombstone	William Clanton Tom & Frank McLaury killed. Morgan & Virgil Earp wounded.
Attack on Benson Stage	Dec. 15, 1881	Malcom's Water Station, 4 miles from Tombstone on Contention Rd.	Attempt on Clum's life, "Whistling Dick" wounded in leg.
Assault on Virgil Earp.	Dec. 28, 1881	5th & Allen Sts. Tombstone.	Deputy U. S. Marshal Virgil Earp wounded.
Murder of Morgan Earp.	March 18, 1882	Campbell & Hatch's Saloon, Allen St.	Morgan Earp killed. Shot in back.
Shooting of Frank Stilwell	March 20, 1882	Tucson rail yards	Stilwell killed by Earp posse.
Shooting at Pete Spence's wood camp.	March 22, 1882	South Pass in the Dragon Mountains.	Florentino killed by Earp posse.

| Fight at Mescal Springs | March 24, 1882 | Mescal Springs, Whetstone Mountains. | Curly Bill & Johnny Barnes killed by Wyatt Earp. |
| Shooting of Warren Earp. | July 6, 1900 | Headquarter's Saloon Willcox, Az. | Warren Earp killed by John N. Boyette. |

3. Wyatt would have been surprised to know that Kate had outlived him. She was born in Budapest, Hungary, on or about, November 7, 1850; and died in the Pioneer's Home in Prescott, Arizona, on November 2, 1940. At the time of her death she was using the name of Mrs. Mary K. Cummings, and was almost ninety years old. For a more complete story of *Big Nose Kate*, see: A. W. Bork and Glenn G. Boyer, Editors, "The O.K. Corral Fight: A Footnote by Kate Elder." *Arizona and the West*, Spring 1977, pp. 65-84.

4. Although he made the claim on a number of occasions, Wyatt Earp was never the Marshal of Dodge City, Kansas. In Earp's favor, however, it can be said that the term *city marshal* was used rather loosely in western towns during the 1870s. Many policemen were referred to as "the city marshal."

The Dodge City *Times* of October 14, 1876, listed Earp as Deputy City Marshal in its "Official Directory." The same listing can be found in the March 25, and March 31, 1877, issues of the same paper. The January 22, 1878, *Ford County Globe* noted that "Wyatt Earp, our old assistant marshal, is at Fort Clark, Texas." Pointing out the good work that Earp had done for the Dodge City Police force, the *Globe* of May 14, 1878, reported: "Wyatt Earp, one of the most efficient officers Dodge ever had, has returned from Fort Worth, Texas. He was immediately appointed Assistant Marshal, by our city dads, much to their credit."

It should be added that there are newspaper and documentary accounts in Dodge City that name Wyatt Earp as the City Marshal. On June 11, 1878, the *Ford County Globe* felt that "Marshal Earp deserves credit for his endeavors to stop the bean business at the threatre the other night." [The bean business being the game of hitting threatre patrons on the heads with beans propelled by blowguns made from soda straws.] It was a game that was almost impossible to stop in a darkened threatre.

Then too, a petition circulated in Dodge City in 1881 to be used for Earp's defense against murder charges brought by Ike Clanton at the conclusion of the "O. K. Corral" fight referred to him as city marshal:

To all whom these presents may come, Greetings: We the undersigned citizens of Dodge City, Ford County, Kansas, and vicinity, do, by these presents certify that we are personally acquainted with Wyatt Earp late of this city; that he came here in the year 1876; that during the years 1877, 1878, and 1879, he was Marshal of our city: . . .

The cowboy participants in the O. K. Corral fight ate breakfast here at the Chandler Milk Ranch the morning before the shootout. Later, Billy Breakenridge shot Billy Grounds from behind the cottonwood tree on left on about March 26, 1882.

Wyatt Earp was giving himself the best of it when he claimed to be city marshal of Dodge City; but many people considered him to be the marshal because he was in the field and made many of the arrests.

The description of a "typical" arrest in Dodge City is told in a letter to Mr. Cruickshanks (father of D. H. Cruickshanks of London, England) from S. D. Allen, March 1938: [spelling and punctuation printed as in the original].

Well to get to Wyatt Earp. My father first mentioned Earp when I gave him the book of Stuart Lake Wyatt Earp Frontier Marshal. I had read the book and found it fascinating but unbelievable and passed it on to the old man to read. As soon as he saw it he grinned and said Oh Yes I remember him . . .

I will conclude this letter by relating to you the only story father ever told me which concerns Wyatt Earp as a marshal in Dodge City. He told me the story about five years ago and said it was a typical arrest. My father and a group of friends were gathered around a billiard table watching a game when Wyatt entered the room and pointed at one of the number, saying that he wanted him. The man approached Earp and they talked for awhile and then Earp swung him around searched him, taking a knife and a number of shotgun cartridges from him. Earp then pushed him towards the door and the cowboy spun about and returned the compliment whereupon Earp punched him in the face and dragged him towards the street, on the sidewalk the prisoner began to struggle telling Earp to let go and cursing him loudly soon they were fighting and Earp butted the man then tripped him, sending him sprawling into the street. Before he got up Earp cracked him over the head with his revolver opening a deep gash. Once the battered drover was in the city jail Earp and another policeman returned to the billiard hall and searched everyone present including my father but found nothing. A doctor had to be called to the jail to attend to the prisoners head and friends of the cowboy my father was one, complained to the mayor about Earp's treatment of his prisoner but got the brush off . . .

I am not suggesting that Earp was a bully he seems to have been a very brave and intelligent man but I am pointing out to you that the reason he lasted so long was because he knew better than to allow his adversaries to get the upperhand . . . . .

My father never did think much of the Dodge police but I believe he was always honest and fair so you can believe me.

Very truly,
S. D. Allen

Wyatt Earp served as a Dodge City peace officer during three periods, "May 17 to September 9, 1876; July 6 to late November, 1877; and May 12, 1878, to September 8, 1879." [Stanley Vestal, *Dodge City: Queen of the Cow Towns*, p. 143]. This schedule agreed with items that appeared in the local newspapers and the dates that Wyatt himself gave. In total, Earp served about 24 months during these three hitches with the Dodge City police force. He was off duty more than six months during 1877 and 1878, which time he used for his Texas trip.

5. It may be true that Earp was hunting for cattle thieves when he made this 1877 trip through Texas; but more likely his first business was the gambling circuit and detective work was a sideline. Wyatt had done work as a private officer in Wichita in 1874. The Wichita *City Eagle* of October 29, 1874, reported the following:

The Higgenbottom outfit, who attempted to jump the county at an expense of twenty or thirty thousand dollars to Wichita, it appears had, among other games, struck M. R. Moser for a new wagon, who instead of putting himself in communication, by telegraph, with the outside world just got two officers, John Behrens and Wiatt [*sic*] Earp, to light out upon the trail. These boys fear nothing and fear nobody. They made about seventy-five miles from Sun to Sun, across trackless prairies, striking the property and the thieves near the Indiana line. To make a long and exciting story short, they just levelled a shotgun, and six-shooter upon the scalawags as they lay concealed in some brush, and told them to "dough over," which they did to the amount of $146, one of them remarking that he was not going to die for the price of a wagon. It is amusing to hear Moser tell how slick the boys did the work.

Since Earp was not appointed to the Wichita police force until April, 1875, (*Proceedings of the Governing Body*. Records of the city of Wichita, Journal B, pp. 44-53, and, Wichita *Weekly Beacon*, April 28, 1875,) it is not likely that he was anything but a special or private officer of some sort. John Behrens, Earp's partner, was a member of the police force at this time; but since he was working so far from the city limits, it is likely that he was also doing private work.

6. The Ed Bailey story has been told by both Wyatt Earp and Kate Elder in situations widely separated by time and geography. Wyatt himself admitted that his story of the affair was secondhand when he explained to the reporter "as it was related to me afterwards." His informant was either the "Hollidays," or Bat Masterson. It is probable that the story is basically true, but *no court nor newspaper records have been found that will substantiate the killing of Ed Bailey in Fort Griffin.* The only court case against Holliday found in Texas is Number 34, the State of Texas vs. Mike Lynch & Dock [sic] Holliday. The following is written by hand across the docket: "Playing together and with each other at a game with cards in a house in which spiritous liquors were sold." The docket is filed in the Shackelford County Courthouse, Albany, Texas. Apparently Holliday left town rather than face the wrath of the court.

Whatever the truth of the affair may be, the rescue of Doc Holliday from the "clutches" of the Fort Griffin law as carried out by Big Nose Kate has become a classic Western theme. Almost every writer and motion picture producer who has done "horse opera" has used it. Broken down into its basic elements the plot usually has the following parts:

a. *The capture*: (Holliday arrested by Fort Griffin marshal).
b. *The victim held in jeopardy:* (threat of mob lynching, or the gallows).
c. *Observation of the plight of the prisoner* by hero or heroine. (Kate views Holliday from back window of the hotel).
d. *The decoy:* (Kate sets fire to the shed to divert attention from Holliday).
e. *The chase*: (Holliday and Kate escape on the horses she has provided).
f. *Sanctuary:* (Holliday and Kate reach safety in Dodge City).

Whatever the facts of the Ed Bailey story may be, Doc and Kate settled in Dodge City for a short time and he commenced to practice dentistry as the following advertisement from the Dodge City *Times* of June 8, 1878, indicates:

Dentistry
J. H. Holliday, Dentist, very respectfully
offers his professional servies to the citizens
of Dodge City and surrounding country during
the summer. Office at room no. 24, Dodge House.
Where satisfaction is not given money will be
refunded.

7. This, no doubt, refers to the killing of Ed Masterson, who was the marshal of Dodge at the time of his death. Larry Deger had been dismissed on December 4, 1877, and Ed Masterson appointed to the position. This change in the city police force was reported by the Dodge City *Times* of December 8, 1877:

On motion of John Newton the office of City Marshal was declared vacant, the Mayor thereupon appointed Edward J. Masterson to the said Marshalship, which appointment the council confirmed.

Since Earp was on his Texas trip at this time, it is obvious that he was not city marshal and had not appointed Masterson as his deputy.

Furthermore, the *Times* of December 15, 1877, states that Charles E. Bassett, Sheriff of Ford County, was named assistant to Ed Masterson.

On April 9, 1878, Ed Masterson, the Marshal of Dodge City, was killed by two drunken Texas drovers. In his later years Bat circulated a story claiming to have avenged his brother's death by personally shooting down the killers. (See, Alfred Henry Lewis, *The Sunset Trail*, pp. 133-139.) Contemporary sources, however, reveal the fact that it was Ed himself who killed Jack Wagner and seriously wounded Alfred Walker. This happened after Ed Masterson was mortally wounded. The Dodge City *Times* of April 13, 1878, ran the following story about the incident:

THE PISTOL
Murder of Edward J. Masterson City Marshal.
The Assailants Shot——One of them Dead.
Dodge City In Mourning.

On Tuesday evening, about 10 o'clock, Edward J. Masterson, Marshal of Dodge City, was murdered by Jack Wagner and Alf Walker, two cattle drivers from near Hays City. The two cow boys were under the influence of bad whiskey and were carrying revolvers. Early in the evening Marshal Masterson disarmed Wagner; later Marshal Masterson and Deputy Marshal Nat Haywood tried the second time to disarm Wagner. While in the act Masterson was shot in the abdomen. Walker in the meantime snapped a pistol in the face of Officer Haywood. Masterson fired four shots, one of them striking Wagner in the bowels from the left side. Walker was struck three times, one shot in the lungs and his right arm horribly shattered with the other shots . . .

8. This is a good description of Holliday, and it has been used by numerous writers. No one has ever doubted that he was quick with a six-shooter and willing to fight, but his accuracy with a revolver has come under question—especially when he was drunk. The Los Angeles *Daily Commercial* of October 15, 1880, printed the following story:

About 12:30 on Sunday night (October 11) a shooting took place at the Oriental Saloon, corner of Fifth and Allen Streets, Tombstone, between M. E. Joyce, one of the proprietors, and a man named Doc Holliday, during the course of which Joyce was shot in the right hand and his partner, Mr. Parker, received a bullet in the big toe.

A more complete account of the affray appeared in the October 12, 1880, edition of the Tombstone *Nugget* under the heading:

> Sunday night a dispute arose in the Oriental Saloon between John Tyley [sic] and Doc Holliday, two well-known sports, and a scene of bloodshed was imminent. Mutual friends disarmed both, and Tyler went away. Holliday remained at the saloon. M. E. Joyce, one of the proprietors, remonstrated with Holliday about creating a disturbance in the saloon and the conversation resulted in Holliday being fired out by Joyce. The former came in and demanded his pistol from behind the bar, where it had been placed by the officer who had disarmed him. It was not given to him and he went out, but in a short time returned and walked toward Joyce, who was just coming from behind the bar, and with a remark that would not look good in print, turned loose with a self cocker. Joyce was not more than ten feet away and jumped for his assailant and struck him over the head with a six-shooter, felling him to the floor and lighting on the top of him. Officers White and Bennett were near at hand and separated them, taking the pistols from each. Just how many shots were fired none present seemed able to tell but in casting up accounts Joyce was found to be shot through the hand, his partner, Mr. Parker, who was behind the bar, shot through the big toe of the left foot, and Holliday with a blow of the pistol in Joyce's hands. . . . .

For his part in the affray Holliday was fined $20 for assault and battery and costs of $11.25.

Doc Holliday's lack of accuracy with a pistol is also demonstrated by his shooting scrape with William Allen in Leadville, Colorado, on August 19, 1884. In *Document no. 258, State of Colorado, vs. John Holliday (alias) Doc Holliday* we see an intoxicated Holliday at 5 p.m. missing his first shot at Allen's head from very close range. His second shot, fired by reaching over the tobacco counter in Hyman's Saloon, hit Allen in the left arm as he lay on the floor. Meaning to make his third shot a fatal one, Doc ran around the counter and placed his *self-cocker* against the prostrate Allen's head; but before he was able to pull the trigger he was disarmed.

There is little doubt that Holliday's poor markmanship was directly related to his state of intoxication.

9. This story is probably basically factual, but no evidence has been found that Holliday shot anyone in Dodge City.

10. Doc and Kate soon tired of life in Dodge City and moved on to greener pastures in Las Vegas, New Mexico. Here the quarrelsome couple settled down and Doc opened a saloon on Center Street. Just when the "Hollidays" left Dodge City is difficult to determine, but his arrest for gambling in March of 1879 occurred six months before Wyatt's arrival in Las Vegas. (*Case no. 990, The Territory of New Mexico, vs. John Holliday*). Apparently he was adjudged "not guilty" of "keeping a gambling table" as the *Records of the District Court, Territory of New Mexico, San Miguel County*, page 121, indicate:

> It is therefore considered and adjudged by the Court that this cause be and the same is hereby dismissed, and that the said defendant John Holladay [sic] as to this prosecution go hence without delay and recover of the said plaintiff his costs in this behalf. . . . .

Hyman's Saloon in Leadville, Colorado, where Doc Holliday shot it out in 1884 with Billy Allen. The cause of the fight originated with a five dollar loan Allen made to Holliday. (Turner-Oster Collection)

The Index to Criminal Papers, San Miguel County, New Mexico Territory, further shows that Holliday was also charged with Case no. 931 and 996, in Las Vegas at about this time, but no details of these charges have been found to date.

Further confirmation of the fact that Doc Holliday left Dodge City well ahead of Wyatt Earp is found in a deed dated July 30, 1879. This instrument filed in the office of the San Miguel County Clerk, Las Vegas, New Mexico, reads in part:

> . . . . .all of the following described lot or parcel of land and real estate situate [sic] and lying and being in the County of San Miguel and Territory of New Mexico to wit: 8 feet of lot 3 (three) block 7 (seven) journing [sic] the saloon of W. Heseran on the east side and the boundary known as the *Holliday Saloon* on the west.

Also contained in this deed is information that shows that his "wife" was with him at this time. The Justice of the Peace, H. G. Neill (Hoodoo Brown) in his instructions and admonitions to the buyer, added:

. . . . J. H. Holliday to me well and personally known as the same person whose names [*sic*] are subscribed to the foregoing deed and as party thereto acknowledges that he signed, sealed, and delivered the said instrument of writing as his free and voluntary act, for the uses and purposes therein set forth, and the said J.. H. Holliday being first by me informed of the contents of the instrument did confess upon separate examination independent and apart of his said wife that he executed the same voluntary and with [*sic*] the compulsion or illicit influence of his said wife.

Holliday and Kate's stay in Dodge must have been short. Doc's arrest (March, 1879) shows that he had been in Las Vegas for at least six months before Wyatt and James left Dodge City (about September 5, 1879). In any case, Wyatt did not leave Dodge City with Doc, nor did Doc pick up Kate in Las Vegas; she was with Holliday when he arrived in Las Vegas.

11. Regardless of what Wyatt Earp said, this is another example of him giving himself the best of it. It was Virgil Earp, Wyatt's older brother, who took the Deputy U. S. Marshalship to Tombstone from Prescott in 1879. This commission, which is on file at the Arizona Historical Society, reads:

Territory of Arizona |
County of Yavapai | ss.
          Pima |

I, V. W. Earp do solemnly swear that I will support the Constitution of the United States and the laws of this territory; That I will in true faith and allegiance bear to the same, and defend them against all enemies, whatsoever; and that I will faithfully and impartially discharge the duties of the office of Deputy United Marshal according to the best of my abilities, so help me God.

(Signed) V. W. Earp

Sworn and subscribed before me this 27th day of November A.D. 1879.

(Name indecipherable)
U. S. District Court.

In addition to Virgil's appointment, Commissions were found in the Arizona Historical Society for Leslie F. Blackborn (appointed March 15, 1881,) and Charles Cushman (appointed December 22, 1881). All three of these federal officers were appointed before Wyatt Earp was given the job on December 29, 1881. Wyatt took over the job when his brother's left arm was shattered by shotgun pellets. See the Tombstone Daily *Nugget*, January 3, 1882, which says:

Wyatt Earp has received the appointment of Deputy United States Marshal, vice, Virgil Earp. Marshal Dake telegraphed the appointment ment upon receipt of the news of Virgil's injuries. So says the Phoenix *Gazette*.

12. The extent and duration of Earp's partnership in the Oriental gaming rooms is not clear. Although on a number of occasions he said his job was that of keeping the peace, or in the language of the day, serving as "bouncer." Wyatt was good at this kind of a job because of his ability with his fists and a gun. A business card, in the possession of Don Shumar of Tombstone, lists three men as heading the gambling concession at the Oriental in 1881: W. Erp [sic], R. B. Clark, and Rickabaugh. The trio did business under a license issued by the City of Tombstone to Rickabaugh & Company (City License Book No. 1). Virgil Earp's testimony at the Spicer Hearing substantiates Wyatt's claim with the following statement:

Wyatt Earp had been sworn in to act in my place while I was in Tucson, and on my return his saloon was opened and I appointed him a "special," to keep the peace, with power to make arrests . . ." (Transcript of Testimony," Document no. 94, Territory of Arizona vs. Morgan Earp, et al, defendants, Deposition of Virgil Earp.)

It is interesting to note that the saloon part of the Oriental was operated by M. E. Joyce and William C. Parker, Jr. and the firm did business under a license issued by the city to Joyce & Company.

The city council appointed Buckskin Frank Leslie a deputy sheriff with power to keep the peace and make arrests in the Oriental Saloon. See, *Minute Book* Common Council, Village of Tombstone, p. 24.

Monday, November 29, 1880: On motion of Comstock seconded by Jones, Frank Leslie was granted power of arrest on the premises of the Oriental Saloon.

13. Wyatt Earp worked about eight months as a Wells Fargo shotgun messenger, giving up the job when he received the appointment as deputy sheriff for Pima County. The Weekly *Nugget* of July 28, 1880, reported:

Sheriff Shibell has appointed Wyatt Earp Deputy Sheriff for this precinct.

For some unknown reason, almost three months after the Shibell appointment, the October 20, 1880, *Epitaph* printed the following report of the incident:

. . . . He (Wyatt) is at present filling the position of shotgun messenger for Wells Fargo & Co., which he will resign to receive the latter appointment.
Morgan Earp succeeds his brother as the shotgun messenger for Wells, Fargo & Co.

Virgil Earp's tenure as city marshal for Tombstone is recorded in *Minute Book No. 1*, Common Council Village of Tombstone by the following entries:

October 28, 1880, pp. 9-10:

Moved by Comstock that Virgil Earp be appointed assistant marshal of the village (substitute for Marshal Fred White) with a salary of $100.00 per month and whose bond shall be placed at $5,000 and whose duty should be to perform all the duties now encumbent upon the present village marshal.

November 15, 1880, p. 18:

Resignation of V. W. Earp Assistant Marshal introduced and accepted.

June 6, 1881, pp. 78-79:

On motion Chief of Police Sippy was granted two weeks leave of absence.
On motion Virgil Earp was appointed Chief of Police during absence of Sippy . . .

Three weeks later, when City Marshal Ben Sippy did not return from his leave of absence, Virgil Earp was made permanent Chief of Police.

June 28, 1881, p. 80:

On motion of Gray V. W. Earp was appointed Chief of Police no dissenting votes.

Virgil Earp's removal as police chief occurred at a council meeting following the "O. K. Corral" shooting with the following temporary order. It is interesting to note that Earp was never permanently removed from office, although he never served after the gunfight.

October 29, 1881, p. 131:

Mayor stated that meeting was called to consider grave charges against Chief of Police Earp and it was ordered that pending investigation of said charges chief Earp be temporarily suspended and James Flyn act as chief during such suspension.

Virgil Earp served a total of 163 days (five months and thirteen days) as Chief of Police of Tombstone.
14. Virgil Earp's description of the arrest of Ike Clanton is more detailed than that given here by Wyatt Earp. See, *Document No. 94*, Territory of Arizona vs. Morgan Earp, et al, Deposition of Virgil Earp:

I found Ike Clanton on 4th Street between Fremont and Allen with a Winchester rifle in his hand and a six-shooter stuck down in his breeches. I walked up and grabbed the rifle in my left hand. He let loose and started to draw his six-shooter. I hit him over the head with mine and knocked him to his knees and took his six-shooter from him.
I asked him if he was hunting for me. He said he was, and if he had seen me a second sooner he would have killed me. I arrested Ike for carrying firearms, I believe was the charge, inside the city limits.

The official record of this arrest of Ike Clanton is contained in

Justice A. O. Wallace's Docket Book: *Recorders Docket*, City of Tombstone, Book No. 1, 1881-1886.

Case No. 106, October 26, 1881,

The Mayor and Common Council of the City of Tombstone
vs
Ike Clanton

Complaint laid before me by Chief of Police Earp charging defendant with carrying concealed weapons. Defendant arrested and brought into court by said officer and pleaded guilty and after due deliberation had thereof, it is ordered, decreed, and adjudged that the defendant pay a fine of $25.00 and costs of this action. Fine and costs paid, and defendant discharged.

A. O. Wallace, Recorder.

15.   Wyatt Earp's story of the arrival of the "cowboys" in Tombstone on October 26, 1881, is not entirely correct. They did not "gallop" into town in a group in answer to a telegram sent by Ike Clanton to Charleston. They were rounding up cattle in the Sulphur Springs Valley at a watering hole called Antelope Springs. On the morning of the 25th they had breakfast at the nearby milk ranch of Jack Chandler. After eating, the group split up with Ike Clanton and Tom McLaury driving a wagon into Tombstone for supplies, while Billy Clanton and Frank McLaury remained to round up cattle near Stockton Hill. While seated at the rancher's table, the "cowboys" arranged an early afternoon meeting on the 26th at the Grand Hotel Bar in Tombstone.

Much of this action is verified in *Document No. 94*, The Territory of Arizona vs. Morgan Earp, et al, Deposition of Ike Clanton:

Q. On what day and at what time of day did you arrive in Tombstone from your ranch prior to the 26th of October 1881?

A. I came in town on the 25th day of October. I think it was between 10 or 11 o'clock in the morning. I did not come from my ranch. I came from Sulphur Springs Valley. I left my ranch three days before that.

Q. Who went with you from your ranch to Sulphur Springs Valley?

A. I went by myself, alone.

Q. Who came in with you from the Sulphur Springs Valley?

A. Tom McLaury.

Q. Did you or did Tom McLaury, to your knowledge, on the night of the 25th or 26th of October, send, or cause to be sent, a telegraphic dispatch from the office here to Charleston or any other point, to William Clanton or Frank McLaury or to any person or persons, directing Frank McLaury or William Clanton to come to Tombstone?

Wyatt Talks   25

A. I did not, and I know that Tom did not, for we had taken breakfast with Frank McLaury and William Clanton the day we came into town (25th), at Jack Chandler's milk ranch, which is ten miles from here, at the foot of the Dragoon Mountains.

. . . .

A. His (Tom's) Winchester was in the stable on Fremont Street below where the shooting occurred. I don't know where his other arms were. (West End Corral).

Q. *Did you come into town with Tom McLaury, and if so, how long before the shooting?*

A. Yes sir, I came into town with him on the day previous to the shooting, it was about 11 o'clock in the forenoon. We came in a spring wagon.

. . . .

Q. *At what time of the day of the shooting did Frank McLaury and Billy Clanton arrive in town?*

A. They arrived in town about half an hour before they were killed. (About 1:30 to 2 p.m.).

Q. *Where did they come from?*

A. They came from Antelope Springs. They are east of here and about thirteen miles from town.

16. Even today, the location of the so-called "O. K. Corral" gun-fight remains a mystery to many historical students and writers. THE SHOOTING DID NOT TAKE PLACE IN THE O. K. CORRAL. The fight actually started on the east fifteen feet of lot number 2, block number 17. On October 26, 1881, this lot belonged to W. A. Harwood and was bounded on the east by Fly's buildings, and on the west by the small Harwood house, a private residence. The Fremont Street entrance to the corral, often designated as the location of the fight by old-timers, is some ninety feet east of this location. The legal description of this "alleyway" is "the west fifteen feet of lot number 6, block 17. THE FIGHT TOOK PLACE ON THE VACANT SPACE ON LOT NUMBER 2, NEXT TO FLY'S ROOMING HOUSE, probably because Doc Holliday was rooming there. There is no doubt that the cowboys, at least Ike Clanton, were laying for him. Their game was broken up by the appearance of Sheriff Behan and the Earps. This is confirmed by a manuscript written by Kate "Holliday" while she was a guest of the Pioneers' Home in Prescott, Arizona (A. W. Bork and Glenn G. Boyer, "The O. K. Corral Fight at Tombstone: A Footnote by Kate Elder," *Arizona and the West*, Spring, 1977, pp. 78-80).

This is commonly called the O. K. Corral fight, which is wrong. The Clantons put their horses at the O. K. Stables, which was on Allen

Street. The Corral was back of it. From this corral was a vacant lot facing clear to Freemont [sic] Street. This duel was fought on this vacant lot about eight feet from the pavement on Freemont [sic] Street.... The Clanton party went through the O. K. Corral. The Earp party came on Freemont [sic] Street.

... Doc left me at his room and went with Morgan at 10:30 p.m. when we got back. I didn't see Doc again until 12:30 a.m. Next morning I got up before he did. I went into the galery [sic] and was looking at the pictures when I saw a man come in with a rifle. He looked in the galery [sic] and went to the dining. After he left, the Mrs. came and said, "Ike Clanton is looking for Doc." I went to our room and said, "Doc, Ike Clanton was here looking for you and had a rifle with him." ... In a little more than a half an hour the shooting began. This lady-friend [Mrs. Fly] and I went to the side window, which faced the vacant lot. One shot went through the window, just two panes above us. My friend left the window, but I stayed there until the fight was over.

17. The "O. K. Corral" fight has been described many times by many witnesses, usually in an inaccurate manner. The intent of these people may have been good, but the action occurred in a brief flash of time, too fast for the human eye and brain to record in its entirety. In many cases, the partisan attitude of the witnesses resulted in deliberately distorted accounts.

Wyatt Earp's description of the fight, like the stories given by the other participants and "witnesses," was also subject to inaccuracies: after all, he had considerable property to lose; was an unwilling participant in the melee; his life was at stake as a result of the Spicer Hearing; and he was carefully advised on what to say by his attorney, Thomas Fitch. Although he was a sworn witness, Earp read his statement from a prepared paper and for some reason was not subjected to cross-examination. The staff of defense attorneys realized that both Doc Holliday and Morgan Earp would make poor witnesses so they were not called to the stand to prevent cross-examination by prosecution lawyers. Morgan Earp had the reputation of being a hothead where fighting was concerned, and Doc Holliday had already demonstrated his quarrelsome nature to the townspeople. "I shot Frank McLaury and Morgan Earp shot Billy Clanton," said Wyatt Earp; but many of the witnesses who were close enough to see testified that Doc Holliday and Morgan Earp opened the fight. From *Document No. 94*, Territory of Arizona vs. Morgan Earp, et al, Defendants:

DEPOSITION OF WILLIAM ALLEN:

I think it was Holliday who fired first. Their backs were to me. I was behind them. The smoke came from him. I could not tell who fired the second shot.......

DEPOSITION OF WESLEY FULLER:

He goes on to say he thinks Morgan Earp and Doc Holliday fired the first shots, but can't tell who fired first.

William Sutherland's three-story hotel in Lamar,
Missouri, where Wyatt met his first wife, Urilla
Sutherland.

DEPOSITION OF WILLIAM CLAIBORNE:

     ..... Then the shooting commenced, right then, in an instant, by Doc Holliday and Morgan Earp . . . . .

Q. *What kind of a pistol did he* [Holliday] *have in his hand?*

A. A nickle-plated pistol.

Q. *Who, in the Earp party, shot first?*

A. Doc Holliday.

Q. *Who shot second?*

A. Morgan Earp.

DEPOSITION OF JOSEPH I. CLANTON:

     The first two shots were fired by Holliday and Morgan Earp. . . . Morgan Earp shot William Clanton and I don't know which one of the McLowery [sic] boys Holliday shot at. He shot at one of them.

DEPOSITION OF JOHN H. BEHAN:

. . . . I saw a nickel-plated pistol in particular which was pointed at one of the party. I think at Billy Clanton. My impression at the time was that Holliday had the nickel-plated pistol.

After the remark, 'Throw up your hands!' was made, the nickel-plated pistol went off.

In order to understand the reasons that triggered the fight, it is necessary to realize that there were divided intentions on the part of both the Earp party of city officers and the cowboys. Wyatt and Virgil wanted to remain in town maintaining *status quo* because they were successful business men who owned perhaps a dozen mining claims, numerous town lots, and valuable water rights. Wyatt had a number of gambling games in town that were making money, and he wanted to be county sheriff. Virgil also was satisfied with his positions of Chief of Police and Deputy U. S. Marshal. Both men probably intended to arrest the cowboys, manhandle them a bit as they had done in the case of Ike Clanton earlier in the day. Neither Wyatt nor Virgil had anything to gain by a shooting scrape at this time.

With Doc and Morgan, however, this was not true. They had no attachments to Tombstone: and, in fact, they preferred Benson and Tucson as bases of operations for their gambling. To make matters worse, they were mad at the cowboys and had made up their minds to carry the fight to them. Mrs. King, in her testimony before the Coroner's Inquest, *Document No. 48*, revealed this intention:

. . . . Then I stepped back into the shop again. The butcher was in the act of cutting the meat when someone at the door said, 'There they come!' and I stepped to the door and looked up the sidewalk and I saw four men coming down the sidewalk. I only knew one of the party and that was Mr. Holliday. And there were three other gentlemen, who someone told me were the Earps. Mr. Holliday was next to the buildings, on the inside. He had a gun under his coat. The way I noticed the gun was that his coat would blow open, and he tried to keep it covered. I stood in the door until these gentlemen passed and until they got to the second door. And what frightened me and made me run back, *I heard this man on* [the] *outside—*[he] *looked at Holliday and I heard him say, 'Let them have it!' And Doc Holliday said, 'All right.'* Then I thought I would run, and [I] ran towards the back of the shop . . . .

There were "divided intentions" in the ranks of the cowboys as well. The preceding twenty-four hours had been a continuous round of gambling and drinking for Ike Clanton and Tom McLaury with little, or no, sleep. To add to their poor condition, both men had been the recipients of Earp wrath by separate "buffaloeing" incidents. Much of their desire to "fight it out," which had been strong the night before, was gone; but Frank McLaury and Billy Clanton, well-rested and sober, were ready to take vengeance on these "city dudes" who had struck down their brothers.

The actual fight was brief and deadly. Virgil Earp had later testified. *Document No. 94*, Territory of Arizona vs. Morgan Earp et al, Deposition of Virgil Earp:

As soon as I saw them, I said, 'Boys, throw up your hands, I want your guns,' or 'arms.' With that, Frank McLowry [sic] and Billy Clanton drew their six-shooters and commenced to cock them, and [I] heard them go "click-click." Ike Clanton threw his hand in his breast, this way [illustrates]. At that, I said throwing both hands up, with the cane in my right hand, 'Hold on, I don't want that!'

Few have guessed, even today, that when Virgil cried, "Hold on" that he was not speaking to the Rustlers, but to his own men to avoid a shooting. Doc and Morgan had gone into action with amazing speed, beating Billy Clanton and Frank McLaury to the draw. Doc had helped his cause with Frank McLaury by shoving the shotgun into the rustler's belly as an attention getting device and then firing his nickel-plated revolver with his right hand. His quick shot struck Frank near his belt buckle. Morgan Earp had reacted almost as fast shooting Billy Clanton in the chest. The rustlers were game, wounding both Virgil and Morgan before they died, but for all practical purposes the fight was over after these first two shots.

Addie Bourland, although not an expert witness, probably gave a better description of the start of the fight than any of the participant witnesses. Her testimony seems to verify the fact that Holliday used the shotgun as a decoy. *Document No. 94*, The Territory of Arizona vs. Morgan Earp, et al., Deposition of Addie Bourland:

I saw first, five men opposite my house, leaning against a small house west of Fly's Gallery and one man was holding a horse, standing a little out from the house. I supposed them to be cowboys, and saw four men coming down the street towards them, and a man with a long coat on walked up to the man holding the horse and put a pistol to his stomach and then he, the man with the long coat on stepped back two or three feet, and the then the firing seemed to be general.

. . . . .
Q. Did you know, or do you know now, the man with the long coat on?

A. I did not know him then. I recognize Doc Holliday, the man sitting there writing, as the man, to the best of my judgement.

. . . . . .
Q. Did you notice the character of weapon Doc Holliday had in his hand?

A. It was a very large pistol.

Q. Did you notice the color of the pistol?

A. It was dark bronze.

Q. Was it or was it not, nickle [sic]-plated pistol?

A. It was not a nickel-plated pistol.

It is quite apparent that Addie Bourland's "very large" bronze pistol was the short-barreled Wells Fargo shotgun. A number of circumstances contributed to her testimony: she knew little about firearms, Holliday's back shielded her view, he held the weapon in one hand (left), and concealed the stock of the gun. *Mrs. Bourland saw only a part of the short barrels.* But with Frank's attention centered on the shotgun, and his actions effectively concealed by his back from the witness, Holliday backed up and fired the nickel-plated pistol with his right hand.

18. The Grand Jury did not act on the charge against the Earps, but Ike Clanton did his best to hang the Earps by filing three separate murder charges against them: October 29, 1881, with Justice Wells Spicer, at Tombstone; February 9, 1882, with Magistrate J. B. Smith at Contention City; and February 15, 1882, with Judge Lucas of Tombstone.

19. See, The Tombstone *Nugget*, January 31, 1882. 3:5&6.
The would-be assassins who attempted to kill Deputy U. S. Marshal Virgil Earp were never brought to justice. After successfully evading Deputy U. S. Marshal Wyatt Earp's posse for almost a month, Ike and Phineas Clanton became tired of hiding and came into Tombstone and surrendered to Sheriff Behan. Sheriff Behan had thoughtfully provided the two cowboys with "protection from the Earps" by appointing a large posse to guard them which was led by Charley Bartholomew and Peter Spencer. [Pete Spence]. The Sheriff and the Clantons were under the impression that the cowboys were wanted for "robbing the U. S. Mail," and had several of their friends ready to swear to a false alibi. They were charged with attempted murder, the specific offense being the shooting of Virgil Earp. The charge did not stick, however, because defense attorneys, Alexander Campbell and Ben Goodrich, pointed out the technicality that the warrant had been served by John H. Jackson, who was not a legally constituted officer and did not have the power to arrest or hold anyone. Since Sheriff Behan and the Courts were "protecting" the cowboys where possible, the case was dropped.
This fancy bit of legal maneuvering backfired for the County Ring, however, and it actually resulted in the death of four cowboys, Frank Stilwell, Florentino, Curly Bill, and John Ringo. The Earp posse killed those accused of the later murder of Morgan Earp, knowing full well that the corrupt courts of Cochise County would turn them loose if they were brought to trial.

20. Wyatt Earp told his friend, John H. Flood, that there were four or five "cowboys" in the Tucson railroad yard that night that Frank Stilwell, one of Morgan Earp's assassins, was killed. "I found him lurking near the train," Wyatt had said, "and he was killed when he grabbed the barrel of my shotgun causing it to discharge." Contemporary newspaper stories, however, mention only Frank Stilwell and Ike Clanton as being there.

Since the Stilwell Inquest is missing from the Pima County courthouse, the story can be told from the Arizona *Weekly Citizen* of April 2, 1881. A synopsis of the testimony of the witnesses follows:

Judge Murphy: He identified the body found near the depot as Frank Stilwell.

Alman J. Hickey: He reported that he saw flashes of gunfire, and a number of men standing where the body was found.

Dr. Dexter Lyford (coroner): He examined Stilwell's body at the undertaker's establishment and found the following wounds:
a. A single ball wound under the armpits passing completely through the body.
b. A rifle ball through upper part of the left arm.
c. A load of buckshot passing through the liver, abdomen, and stomach. This was fired at very close range.
d. A rifle ball through the fleshy section of right leg.
e. A load of buckshot through the left leg.

J. W. Evans: He saw Doc Holliday get off the cars with a shotgun in both hands . . . saw Frank Stilwell at the depot and his coat protruded as if he had a pistol in the pocket.

David Gibson: He saw Wyatt and Warren Earp, Doc Holliday, and a short man (McMasters) walk from Porter's Hotel to the depot. The two Earps had short Wells Fargo shotguns. Holliday had a ulster (heavy overcoat) over his shoulder and a gun under it. He heard two shots quickly followed by five more that seemed to come from the front of the train.

C. T. Brown: He met four men dressed in dark clothes and carrying guns; they were going south towards Camp Street. One man was carrying an overcoat [Holliday].

Nathan W. Waite: He came to Tucson on the same train with Virgil Earp and his wife, Warren Earp, Wyatt Earp, Doc Holliday, and Sherman McMasters. All parties boarded train at Contention City. All had guns and McMasters had two belts of cartridges.

Isaac Clanton: He testified that he knew Frank C. Stilwell who was a native of Texas, aged about 27 years. Stilwell told Ike that the Earps and Holliday were aboard the train. After talking for a few minutes Doc Holliday, McMasters, Johnson, Wyatt and Warren Earp came out of the hotel and walked towards the train. In a few minutes he heard shooting near the front of the train. He later returned from downtown and inquired about the shooting—did not know Stilwell had been killed until this morning.

S. A. Batman: The engineer on train when Stilwell was killed, said he saw a man with a Winchester rifle walking up and down by the side of the train and was told that the man was one of the Earps guarding a party that was going through to California; shortly afterwards saw a man and lady (Virgil and Allie Earp) come out of the hotel, the man had an arm in a sling; two men carrying Winchester rifles walked behind them. They got on the cars, the one outside still looking everywhere.

He saw one of them walking down the track and in a few minutes heard several shots followed by some cheering.

John Hanlon: He left Tombstone [*sic*] [Tucson] on the 20th, boarded train at Benson. When about halfway between Tombstone and Contention, saw the Earp party. [Since the railroad did not run from Contention to Tombstone, Mr. Hanlon must have been on the stage running from Contention to Tombstone]. Some were on horseback and some were in a buggy. Also saw the same party at Contention, all heavily armed. [The Earp party boarded the train for Tucson at Contention].

James Miller: Fireman on westbound train on the evening of the 20th, saw a man running down the track on the east side of the engine and cross the track in front of it. Eight or ten minutes afterwards saw four armed men pass on the west side of the engine and down to the left of the coaches standing on the side track. In about five minutes afterward heard five or six shots fired in rapid succession. Saw one man while they were shooting, but saw four men standing there when the train pulled out. Watched to see if they boarded the train. When they first passed down they all had guns; but when the train ran by a few minutes later the four men were standing where the firing had been done and had no guns in their hands. Saw one man fire a gun. He was a middle-sized man. The shooting was done by the same party who passed the engine. The man who ran down the east side and crossed the tracks had no gun [This was Stilwell and he had a six-shooter]. Heard someone say before this took place that there would be murder done there.

R. E. Mellis: Was engineer on the outgoing train, and while on the lookout for tramps saw a man cross in front of the engine, and shortly afterwards four armed men walked down on the west side of the train to where the man was. Heard them fire. There must have been a dozen shots . . . Heard the firing and saw the flashes of the guns. Saw four men standing where the shooting had been done.

Engineer Clark: Was the engineer on the freight going east (to Contention City) when it was flagged by the Earp party at Papago Station. [After the Stilwell killing the Earps hitched a ride in the caboose and returned to Contention where they picked up their horses and buggy and returned to Tombstone].

21. No incident of early Tombstone history created more controversy than the killing of Curly Bill Brocius by Wyatt Earp at Mescal Springs. Part of the controversy resulted from the fact that the *Epitaph* (March 25, 1882), had scooped the *Nugget*. The *Epitaph* had headlined its report the "Battle of Burleigh." (This location was given to confuse Sheriff Behan as to Earp's real location). While the *Nugget* responded (March 26, 1882), with their version of the fight called "The True Business." Both newspapers agreed that there had been a fight, but the *Nugget* insisted that Curly Bill had not been killed.

In order to counter the *Epitaph's* scoop, the *Nugget* sent couriers to Contention City and Mescal Springs to authenticate, if possible the *Epitaph's* account. Telegrams sent from Charleston at 8:00 p.m. and 8:40 p.m. contained the following information:

a. The Earp party had definitely had a fight in the Whetstone Mountains.

b. Wyatt Earp stood fire and was struck with a ball in the breast.

c. The Earp party rode for cover leaving Wyatt alone.

d. Texas Jack's horse was killed.

e. It is impossible to ascertain anything in regard to Curly Bill.

At this time the *Nugget* and the *Epitaph* were not far apart in reporting the facts of this fight, although the *Nugget* was confident that Earp had either been wounded or killed, and that mystery surrounded the fate of Curly Bill.

The cowboy-Behan rumor mill, however, soon dug up "new facts" about the fight that placed the *Nugget* in the realm of the ridiculous, chief among which were:

a. Curly Bill was not killed at Mescal Springs because he was not there. The party at the springs was Pink Truly and Alex Arnold, tinhorns who had robbed a Charleston store, and two companions.

b. The Earp party had killed an innocent Mexican who happened to have curly black hair, and delivered the head to Henry Hooker in a sack, claiming the $1,000 reward offered for Curly Bill.

c. Earp had worn a steel vest at the Mescal Springs fight—a fact that saved his life from the deadly cowboy fire.

Wild rumors, such as these, circulated by the rustler element of early Tombstone in order to discredit Wyatt Earp are strong evidence that Earp's version of the fight is correct. Well-known writers, nevertheless, such as William Breakenridge and Frank Waters have used these tales in popular books to make Earp appear ridiculous. For example in Waters' *The Earp Brothers of Tombstone*, p. 199.

Hooker's account, as told to Judge Hancock was a little different. He said that when the Earp party arrived at the ranch, one of them rolled out from a sack a black, curly-haired head, demanding the thousand dollar cash reward. Colonel Hooker gave them a laugh and sent them on their way.

In *Helldorado*, Breakenridge writes (page 176-177):

As the Earp party rode up to the spring the four cowboys took refuge behind an embankment, and all but Wyatt of the Earp party turned and rode away. Wyatt, however, rode up rather close to them and dismounted, and with the bridle rein on his arm stepped in front of his horse, raised his rifle and fired at them. They returned the fire. Alex Arnold reported that Earp was wearing a white shirt which made a splendid target. He was only a short distance away and drew a fine bead on Wyatt and fired. Earp turned partly around and staggered back to horse . . . Both Truly and Arnold claimed that Wyatt Earp had a steel vest on under his shirt which deflected the bullet. . . .

To corroborate the story as told by Arnold and Truly, a prominent citizen, now of Tucson, but who at the time was a deputy sheriff

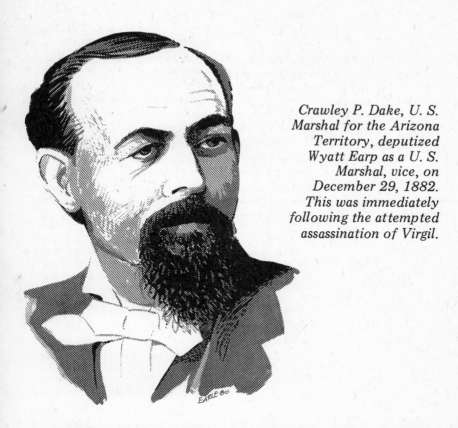

Crawley P. Dake, U. S. Marshal for the Arizona Territory, deputized Wyatt Earp as a U. S. Marshal, vice, on December 29, 1882. This was immediately following the attempted assassination of Virgil.

under Behan, [The Daily *Nugget* of April 1, 1882, shows this deputy to be Frank Herford] was at what is now known as the McKittrick Ranch, about twelve miles north of Willcox, when the Earp crowd were seen in the distance coming towards the ranch. The wife of the ranch owner was very sick, and he asked the deputy to go into the granary out of sight until they got away from there, as he was afraid that if they made any row it would endanger his wife's life. The granary had no window and was very dark, but the door was partly open. The rancher met the Earps as they rode up, explained his wife's condition, and asked them to move on, as he was afraid that if the sheriff's posse came while they were there the excitement would kill his wife. They said that they were very hungry, and if he would give them some supper they would move on as soon as they ate.

While the cook was getting them supper, Wyatt Earp, Doc Holliday, and one other came and stood right at the partially open door of the granary, not three feet away from it. . . and that Earp's overcoat had a bullet hole through each side of the front of it, and he heard one of them say [Doc Holliday], 'The steel saved you that time.'

Asked about this story years later, Wyatt laughed and said, "I wonder if they thought about how hot one of those things would be on the Arizona desert."

22. When word reached Hooker's Ranch that Sheriff Behan was on his way with a posse of twenty-two men, Wyatt led his men to the top of a small hill called Hooker's Butte. "Tell Behan," Earp said to the rancher, "I'll be waiting for him up there. If he wants me real bad to come and get me." The "gallant" Sheriff and his posse of ranchers and rustlers rode to a point near the foot of the hillock, well out of rifle range, and stopped to have a look. It would have required more courage than Behan's men possessed to dislodge the Earps from their hilltop fortress, and the Sheriff and his men wisely rode back to Willcox empty-handed.

23. There was never a serious attempt made to arrest Wyatt Earp in Colorado, although Sheriff Paul did go to Denver with a warrant (about May 18, 1882). By the time Paul arrived in Colorado the Earps were back in Arizona. The May 10, 1882, Tombstone *Nugget* story, "Probably Killed," states:

> It is probably true that the rumor of the death of Wyatt Earp is true. It appears that while the Earp party was in Albuquerque Doc Holliday became intoxicated and indiscreet [*sic*] in his remarks, which offended Wyatt and caused the party to break up. Holliday went with Tipton, and it is said was with him when he was killed. Wyatt returned to Hooker's, of this there is no question, as a citizen of this place saw and talked with him there last week, and it was in that vicinity that he is reported to have been killed. . . .

Holliday was arrested in Denver by bounty hunter, Perry Mallon, and Arizona attempted to extradite him, but the Governor of Colorado refused to sign the papers.

24. Wyatt is wrong here. Doc Holliday died in Glenwood Springs, Colorado, Tuesday, November 8, 1887, about 10:00 a.m. He had never returned to Arizona.

Peter Spence[r] was a member of the cowboy
faction and an alleged participant in the killing
of Morgan Earp at Hatch's Saloon.

Chapter 2

WYATT'S TESTIMONY— O.K. CORRAL INQUEST

Three weeks after the O. K. Corral Shootout a hearing was held before Judge Wells Spicer. Wyatt Earp's testimony before that hearing was in the form of a carefully prepared statement and he was not cross-examined.

In Justice Court, Township No. One, Cochise County, Arizona Territory

Territory of Arizona	
vs.	Deposition
Morgan Earp, et al	

On this 16th day of November 1881, upon the hearing of the above entitled action, on the examination of Wyatt Earp and J. H. Holliday, having first been informed of his right to make a statement, as provided in Section 133, page 22 of the laws of Arizona, approved February 12, 1881, and said Wyatt Earp having chosen to make a statement under oath and having been personally sworn, makes such statement under oath in answer to the interrogatories as follows:

Territory of Arizona	
	ss
County of Cochise	

Q. *What is your name and age?*
A. My name is Wyatt Earp—32 years old last March the 19th.
Q. *Where were you born?*
A. In Monmouth, Warren County, Illinois.

Justice of the Peace, Wells Spicer, was the judge during the O. K. Corral inquest.

Q. *Where do you reside and how long have you resided there?*

A. I reside in Tombstone, Cochise County, Arizona. Since December 1, 1879.[1]

Q. *What is your business and profession?*

A. Saloon keeper at present. Also have been deputy sheriff and also a detective.[2]

Q. *Give any explanation you may think proper of the circumstances appearing in the testimony against you and state any facts which you think will tend to your exculpation.*

A. The difficulty which resulted in the death of William Clanton and Frank and Tom McLoury originated last spring. [Objection made by the counsel for the prosecution against the defendant Wyatt Earp in making his statement, of using a manuscript from which to make such statement, and object to the said defendant being allowed to make statement without limit as to its relevancy. Objection overruled by the court][3] and at a little over a year ago, I followed Tom and Frank McLoury and two other parties who had stolen six government mules from Camp Rucker. Myself, Virgil Earp and Morgan Earp and Marshall Williams, Captain Hurst and four soldiers—we traced those mules to McLoury's ranch.[4] [Here counsel for prosecution moves to strike out the foregoing statement as irrelevant. Objection overruled.]

While at Charleston I met a man by the name of Dave Estes. He told me I would find the mules at McLoury's ranch. He said he had seen them there the day before. He said they were branding the mules "D S," making the D. S. out [of] U.S. We tracked the mules right up to the ranch. Also found the branding iron D.S. Afterwards some of those mules were found with the same brand. After we arrived at McLoury's ranch, there was a man by the name of Frank Patterson. He made some kind of a compromise with Capt. Hurst. Capt. Hurst came to us boys and told us he had made this compromise and by so doing, he would get his mules back. We insisted on following them up. Hurst prevailed on us to go back to Tombstone, and so we came back. Hurst told us two or three weeks afterwards that they would not give up the mules to him after we left, saying that they only wanted to get us away; that they could stand the soldiers off. Capt. Hurst cautioned me and my brothers, Virgil and Morgan, to look out for those men, as they had made some threats against our lives.[5]

About one month after we had followed up those mules, I met Frank and Tom McLoury in Charleston. They tried to pick a fuss out of me down there and told me if I ever followed them up again as close as I did before they would kill me. Shortly after that time Bud Philpot was killed by the men who tried to rob the Benson stage, as a detective I helped trace the matter up, and I was satisfied that three men, named Billy Leonard, Harry Head, and James Crane, were in that robbery. I knew that Leonard, Head, and Crane were friends and associates of the Clantons and McLourys and often stopped at their ranches.

It was generally understood among officers and those who have information about criminals that Ike Clanton was sort of a chief among the Cow Boys; that the Clantons and McLourys were cattle thieves and generally in the secret of the stage robbery; and that the Clantons' and McLourys' ranches were meeting places and places of shelter for the gang.[6]

I had an ambition to be sheriff of this county at the next election, and I thought it would be a great help with the people and business men if I could capture the men who killed Philpot. There were rewards offered of about 1200 dollars each for the capture of the robbers. Altogether there was about 3600 dollars offered for their capture. I thought this sum might tempt Ike Clanton and Frank McLoury to give away Leonard, Head, and Crane. I went to Ike Clanton, Frank McLoury and Joe Hill, when they came in town—I had an interview with them in the back yard of the Oriental Saloon. I told them what I wanted. I told them I wanted the glory of capturing Leonard, Head, and Crane, and if I could do it, it would help me make the race for sheriff at the next election. I told them if they would put me on the track of Leonard, Head, and Crane, and tell me where those men were hid, I would give them all the reward and would never let anyone know where I got the information.

Ike Clanton said that he would like to see them captured. He said that Leonard claimed a ranch that he claimed, and that if he could get him out of the way he would have no opposition in regard to the ranch.[7] Clanton said that Leonard, Head, and Crane would make a fight, that they would never be taken alive, and that I must find out if the reward would be paid for the capture of the robbers dead or alive. I then went to Marshall Williams, the agent of Wells Fargo & Co. in this town, and at my request he telegraphed to the agent or superintendent in San Francisco, to find out if the reward would be paid for the robbers dead or alive. He received, in June, 1881, a telegram, which he showed me, promising the reward would be paid dead or alive.

The next day I met Ike Clanton and Joe Hill on Allen Street in front of a little cigar store next to the Alhambra. I told them that the dispatch had come. I went to Marshall Williams and told him I wanted to see the dispatch for a few minutes. He went to looking for it and could not find it, but went over to the telegraph office and got a copy of it, and he came back and gave it to me. I went and showed it to Ike Clanton and Joe Hill and returned it to Marshall Williams, and afterwards told Frank McLoury of its contents.

It was then agreed between us that they were to have all the 3600 dollars reward, outside of necessary expenses for horse hire in going after them, and that Joe Hill should go to where Leonard, Head, and Crane were hid, over near Yreka, in New Mexico, and lure them in near Frank and Tom McLoury's ranch near

The Mining Exchange Building was the site of the Earp-Holliday hearing that was conducted after the O. K. Corral fight. The courtroom was located on the first floor at the center of the building. (Arizona Historical Society)

Soldier's Holes, 30 miles from here, and I would be on hand with a posse and capture them.

I asked Joe Hill, Ike Clanton, and Frank McLoury what tale they would make them to get them over here. They said they had agreed upon a plan to tell them there would be a paymaster going from Tombstone to Bisbee, to pay off the miners, and they wanted them to come in and take him in. Ike Clanton then sent Joe Hill to bring them in. Before starting, Joe Hill took off his watch and gave it to Virgil Earp to keep for him until he got back. He was gone about ten days and returned with the word that he got there a day too late—that Leonard and Harry Head had been killed the day before he got there by horse thieves. I learned afterwards that the horse thieves had been killed subsequently by members of the Clanton and McLoury gang.

After that, Ike Clanton and Frank McLoury claimed that I had given them away to Marshall Williams and Doc Holliday, and when they came in town they shunned us, and Morgan, Virgil Earp, Doc Holliday, and myself began to hear their threats against us.

I am a friend of Doc Holliday's because when I was city marshal of Dodge City, Kansas, he came to my rescue and saved my life when I was surrounded by desperadoes.

About a month or more ago (October, 1881), Morgan Earp and myself assisted to arrest Stilwell and Spence on the charge of robbing the Bisbee stage. The McLourys and Clantons were always friendly with Spence and Stilwell, and they laid the whole blame of their arrest on us, though the fact is we only went as a sheriff's posse. After we got in town with Spence and Stilwell, Ike Clanton and Frank McLoury came in.

Frank McLoury took Morgan Earp into the street in front of the Alhambra, where John Ringo, Ike Clanton, and the two Hicks boys were also standing. Frank McLoury commenced to abuse Morgan Earp for going after Spence and Stilwell. Frank McLoury said he will never speak to Spence again for being arrested by us. He said to Morgan, "If you ever come after me, you will never take me." Morgan replied that if he ever had occasion to go after him, he would arrest him. Frank McLoury then said to Morgan Earp, "I have threatened you boys' lives, and a few days ago I had taken it back. But since this arrest, it now goes." Morgan made no reply and walked off.

Before this and after this Marshall Williams, Farmer Daly, Ed Byrnes, Old Man Urrides, Charlie Smith, and three or four others had told us of at different times of threats to kill us, made by Ike Clanton, Frank McLoury and Tom McLoury, Joe Hill, and John Ringo. I knew that all those men were desperate and dangerous men—that they were connected with outlaws, cattle thieves, robbers, and murderers. I knew of the McLourys' stealing six government mules, and also cattle, and when the owners went after them, finding his stock on the McLoury boys' ranch, that he was drove off and told that if he ever said anything about it he would be killed, and he kept his mouth shut until several days ago for fear of being killed.

I heard of Ringo shooting a man down in cold blood near Camp Thomas.[8] I was satisfied that Frank and Tom McLoury killed and robbed Mexicans in Skeleton Canyon, about three or four months ago and I naturally kept my eyes open and did not intend that any of the gang should get the drop on me if I could help it.

Ike Clanton met me at Vogan's [Vogan's Bowling Alley] old saloon five or six months ago and told me I had told Holliday about this transaction, of his giving away Head, Leonard, and Crane. I told him I had never told Holliday anything. I told him that when Holliday came up from Tucson I would prove it. Ike said that Holliday had told him so. On the night of the 25th, Holliday met Ike Clanton in the Alhambra lunch room and asked him about it. Clanton denied it. They quarreled for three or four minutes. Holliday told Clanton he was a damned liar, if he said so. I was sitting eating lunch at the lunch counter. Morgan Earp was standing at the Alhambra bar, talking with the bartender. I called him over to where I was sitting, knowing that he was an officer, and told him that Holliday and Clanton were quarreling in the lunch room and for him to go in and stop it. He climbed over the lunch room counter from the Alhambra bar and went into the room, took Holliday by the arm and led him into the street. Ike Clanton in a few seconds followed them out. I got through eating and walked out of the bar. As I stopped at the door of the bar, they were still quarreling.

Just then Virgil came up, I think out of the Occidental, and told them, Holliday and Clanton, if they didn't stop their quarreling he would have to arrest them.[9] They all separated at that time, Morgan Earp going down the street, home; Virgil Earp going into the Occidental saloon; Ike going across the street to the Grand Hotel. I walked in the Eagle Brewery, where I had a faro game which I had not closed. I stayed in there a few minutes and walked out to the street, and there met Ike Clanton. He asked me if I would take a walk with him, that he wanted to talk to me. I told him I would if he did not go too far, as I was waiting for my game in the Brewery to close, and I would have to take care of the money. We walked about halfway down the Brewery building, going down Fifth Street and stopped.

He told me when Holliday approached him in the Alhambra that he wasn't fixed just right. He said that in the morning he would have man-for-man, that this fighting talk had been going on for a long time and he guessed it was about time to fetch it to a close. I told him I would not fight no one if I could get away from it, because there was no money in it. He walked off and left me saying, 'I will be ready for you in the morning.'

I walked over to the Oriental. He followed me in and took a

drink, having his six-shooter in plain sight. He says, 'You must not think I won't be after you all in the morning.' He said he would like to make a fight with Holliday now. I told him Holliday did not want to fight, but only to satisfy him that this talk had not been made. About that time the man that is dealing my game closed it and brought the money to me. I locked it in the safe and started home. I met Holliday on the street between the Oriental and Alhambra. Myself and Holliday walked down Allen Street, he going to his room and I to my house, going to bed.

I got up the next day, October 26, about noon. Before I got up, Ned Boyle came to me and told me that he met Ike Clanton on Allen Street, near the telegraph office; that Ike was armed; that he said, 'As soon as those damned Earps make their appearance on the street today, the ball will open,' that Ike said, 'We are here to make a fight. We are looking for the son of bitches.' I laid in bed some little time after that, and got up and went down to the Oriental saloon.

Harry Jones came to me after I got up, and said, 'What does all this mean?' I asked him what he meant. He says, 'Ike Clanton is hunting you boys with a Winchester rifle and six-shooter.' I said 'I will go down and find him and see what he wants.' I went out, and on the corner of Fifth and Allen I met Virgil Earp, the marshal. He told me how he heard Ike Clanton was hunting us. I went down Allen Street and Virgil went down Fifth Street and then Fremont Street. Virgil found Ike Clanton on Fourth Street near Fremont Street, in the mouth of the alleyway. He walked up to him and said, 'I hear you are hunting for some of us.' I was coming down Fourth Street at this time. Ike Clanton then threw his Winchester rifle around toward Virgil. Virgil grabbed it and hit Ike Clanton with his six-shooter and knocked him down. Clanton had his rifle, and his six-shooter in his pants. By that time I came up. Virgil and Morgan Earp took his rifle and six-shooter and took them to the Grand Hotel after examination and I took Ike Clanton before Justice Wallace. [10]

Before the investigation, Morgan Earp had Ike Clanton in charge, as Virgil Earp was out at that time. After I went into Judge Wallace's court and sat down on a bench, Ike Clanton looked over to me and said, 'I will get even with all of you for this. If I had a six-shooter now I would make a fight with all of you.' Morgan Earp then said to him, 'If you want to make a

Peter Spence[r] lived at this house at First and Fremont Streets. (Turner Collection)

fight right bad, I will give you this one,' at the same time offering Ike Clanton his own six-shooter. Ike Clanton started to get up and take it, when Campbell, the deputy sheriff, pushed him back in his seat, saying he would not allow any fuss. I never had Ike Clanton's arms at any time, as he stated.

I would like to describe the positions we occupied in the courtroom. Ike Clanton sat on a bench with his face fronting to the north wall of the building. I myself sat down on a bench that ran against and along the north wall, in front of where Ike sat. Morgan Earp stood up on his feet with his back against the wall and to the right of where I sat, and two or three feet from me.

Morgan Earp had Ike Clanton's Winchester in his hand, like this, with one end on the floor, with Clanton's six-shooter in his right hand. We had them all the time. Virgil Earp was not in the courtroom during any of this time and came there after I had walked out. He was out, he told me, hunting for Judge Wallace.

I was tired of being threatened by Ike Clanton and his gang, and believe from what he said to me and others and from their movements that they intended to assassinate me the first chance they had, and I thought that if I had to fight for my life with them I had better make them face me in an open fight. So I said to Ike Clanton, who was then sitting about eight feet away from me, 'You damned dirty cow thief. You have been threatening our lives and I know it. I think I would be justified in shooting you down any place I should meet you. But if you are anxious to make a fight, I will go anywhere on earth to make a fight with you—even over to the San Simon, among your own crowd.'

He replied, 'I will see you after I get through here. I only want four feet of ground to fight on.'

I walked out, and just then, outside of the courtroom, near the Justice's office, I met Tom McLoury. He came up to me and said to me, 'If you want to make a fight, I will make a fight with you, anywhere.' I supposed at the time that he had heard what had just transpired between Ike Clanton and myself. I knew of his having threatened me and I felt just as I did about Ike Clanton, and if the fight had to come, I had better have it come when I had an even show to defend myself. So I said to him, 'All right, make a fight right here,' and at the same time slapped him in the face with my left hand and drew my pistol with my right. He had a pistol in plain sight on his right hip, in his pants, but made no move to draw it. I said to him, 'Jerk your gun and use it.' He made no reply and I hit him on the head with my six-shooter and walked away,[11] down to Hafford's corner. I went into Hafford's and got a cigar and came out and stood by the door.

Pretty soon after I saw Tom McLoury, Frank McLoury and William Clanton passed me and went down Fourth Street to the gunsmith shop. I followed down to see what they were going to do. When I got there, Frank McLoury's horse was standing on the sidewalk with his head in the door of the gunshop. I took the horse by the bit, as I was deputy city marshal, and commenced to back him off the sidewalk. Tom and Frank McLoury and Billy Clanton came to the door. Billy Clanton laid his hand on his six-shooter. Frank McLoury took hold of the horse's bridle, and I said, 'You will have to get this horse off the sidewalk.' He backed him off into the street. Ike Clanton came up about this time and they all walked into the gunshop. I saw them in the gunshop changing cartridges into their belts. They came out of the shop and walked along Fourth Street to the corner of Allen Street. I followed them as far as the corner of Fourth and Allen Streets. They went down Allen Street and over to Dubar's corral.

Virgil Earp was then city marshal. Morgan Earp was a special policeman—for six weeks or two months he wore a badge and drew pay. I had been sworn in in Virgil's place to act for him while Virgil was gone to Tucson on Spence's and Stilwell's trial.

*Joseph Isaac Clanton,
observer of the
O. K. Corral
fight and enemy
of the Earps.*

Virgil had been back several days but I was still acting, and I knew it was Virgil's duty to disarm those men. I expected he would have trouble in doing so and I followed up to give assistance if necessary, especially as they had been threatening us, as I have already stated.

About ten minutes afterwards, and while Virgil, Morgan, Doc Holliday, and myself were standing on the corner of Fourth and Allen Streets, persons said, 'There is going to be trouble with those fellows.' And one man named Coleman said to Virgil, 'They mean trouble. They have just gone from Dunbar's corral into the O. K. Corral, all armed, and I think you had better go and disarm them.' Virgil turned around to Holliday, Morgan Earp, and myself and told us to come and assist him in disarming them.

Morgan Earp said to me, 'They have horses. Had we not better get some horses ourselves, so that if they make a running fight we can catch them.' I said, 'No. If they try to make a running fight we can kill their horses and then capture them.'

We four then started through Fourth to Fremont Street. When we turned the corner of Fourth and Fremont we could see them standing near or about the vacant space between Fly's photograph gallery and the next building west. I first saw Frank McLoury, Tom McLoury, Billy Clanton, and Sheriff Behan standing there. We went down the left-hand side of Fremont Street. When I got within about 150 feet of them I saw Ike Clanton and Billy Clanton and another party. We had walked a few steps further and I saw Behan leave the party and come toward us. Every few steps he would look back as if he apprehended danger. I heard him say to Virgil Earp, 'For God's sake, don't go down there, you will get murdered.' Virgil replied, 'I am going to disarm them,'—he, Virgil, being in the lead. When I and Morgan Earp came up to Behan he said, 'I have disarmed them.' When he said this, I took out my pistol, which I had in my hand, under my coat, and put it in my overcoat pocket. Behan then passed up the street and we walked on down.

We came up on them close—Frank McLoury, Tom McLoury, and Billy Clanton standing all in a row against the east side of the opposite side of the vacant space west of Fly's photograph gallery. Ike Clanton and Billy Claiborn and a man I don't know were standing in the vacant space about halfway between the photograph gallery and the next building west.

I saw that Billy Clanton and Frank and Tom McLoury had their hands by their sides. Frank McLoury and Billy Clanton's six-shooters were in plain sight. Virgil said, 'Throw up your hands, I have come to disarm you.' Billy Clanton and Frank McLoury laid their hands on their six-shooters. Virgil said, 'Hold. I don't mean that. I have come to disarm you.' Then Billy Clanton and Frank McLoury commenced to draw their pistols. At the same time, Tom McLoury throwed his hand to his right hip, throwing his coat open like this, and jumped behind his horse. I had my pistol in my overcoat pocket, where I had put it when Behan told us he had disarmed the other parties. I drew my pistol. Billy Clanton levelled his pistol on me, but I did not aim at him. I knew that Frank McLoury had the reputation of being a good shot and a dangerous man, and I aimed at Frank McLoury. The two first shots were fired by Billy Clanton and myself, he shooting at me and I shooting at Frank McLoury. I don't know which was fired first. We fired almost together. The fight then became general.

*Thomas Clark McLaury,
born June 30, 1853, and
died in the O. K. Corral
fight on October 26, 1881.*

After about four shots were fired, Ike Clanton ran up and grabbed my left arm. I could see no weapon in his hand, and thought at the time he had none, and so I said to him, 'The fight has commenced. Go to fighting or get away,'—at the same time pushing him off with my left hand, like this. He started and ran down the side of the building and disappeared between the lodging house and photograph gallery.

My first shot struck Frank McLoury in the belly.[12] He staggered off on the sidewalk, but first fired one shot at me. When we told them to throw up their hands, Claiborn threw up his left hand and broke and ran. I never saw him afterward till late in the afternoon, after the fight. I never drew my pistol or made a motion to shoot until after Billy Clanton and Frank McLoury drew their pistols. If Tom McLoury was unarmed, I did not know it. I believed he was armed and fired two shots at our party before Holliday, who had the shotgun, fired and killed him. If he was unarmed, there was nothing in the circumstances or in what had been communicated to me or in his acts or threats that would have led me even to suspect his being unarmed.

I never fired at Ike Clanton, even after the shooting commenced, because I thought he was unarmed. I believed then, and

Robert Findley (Frank) McLaury, born March 3, 1848, and died October 26, 1881, in the O. K. Corral fight with the Earps.

believe now, from the acts I have stated and the threats I have related and the other threats communicated to me by other persons as having been made by Tom McLoury, Frank McLoury, and Ike Clanton, that these men last named had formed a conspiracy to murder my brothers, Morgan and Virgil, Doc Holliday, and myself. I believe I would have been legally and morally justifiable in shooting any of them on sight. But I did not do so, nor attempt to do so. I sought no advantage when I went as deputy marshal to help disarm them and arrest them. I went as a part of my duty and under the direction of my brother, the marshal. I did not intend to fight unless it became necessary in self-defense and in the performance of official duty. When Billy Clanton and Frank McLoury drew their pistols, I knew it was a fight for life, and I drew and fired in defense of my own life and the lives of my brothers and Doc Holliday.

I have been in Tombstone since December 1, 1879. I came here directly from Dodge City, Kansas. Against the protest of business men and officials, I resigned the office of city marshal, which I held from 1876. I came to Dodge City from Wichita, Kansas. I was on the police force in Wichita from 1874 until I went to Dodge City.[13]

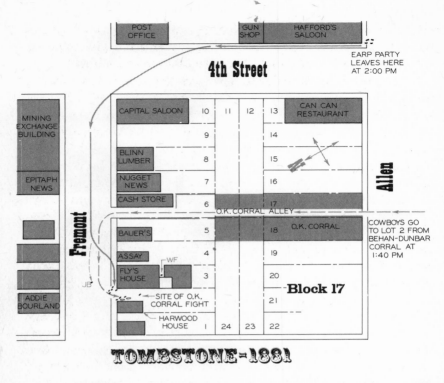

POST OFFICE | GUN SHOP | HAFFORD'S SALOON

EARP PARTY LEAVES HERE AT 2:00 PM

4th Street

MINING EXCHANGE BUILDING

EPITAPH NEWS

ADDIE BOURLAND

Fremont

CAPITAL SALOON | 10 | 11 | 12 | 13 | CAN CAN RESTAURANT

BLINN LUMBER | 9 | | 14

NUGGET NEWS | 8 | | 15

CASH STORE | 7 | | 16

6 | | 17

O.K. CORRAL ALLEY

BAUER'S | 5 | | 18 | O.K. CORRAL

ASSAY | 4 | | 19

WF

FLY'S HOUSE | 3 | | 20

JB

SITE OF O.K. CORRAL FIGHT | | 21

HARWOOD HOUSE | 1 | 24 | 23 | 22

Block 17

Allen

COWBOYS GO TO LOT 2 FROM BEHAN-DUNBAR CORRAL AT 1:40 PM

TOMBSTONE-1881

The boasting of Issac Clanton that I ever said to him that I had anything to do with any stage robbery or giving any information of Morg going on the stage, or any improper communication whatever with any criminal enterprise is a tissue of lies from beginning to end.

Sheriff Behan made me an offer in his office on Allen Street in the back room of a cigar store, where he, Behan, had his office, that if I would withdraw and not try to get appointed sheriff of Cochise County that he would hire a clerk and divide the profits. I done so, and he never said another word to me about it afterwards, but claimed in his statement and gave his reason for not complying with his contract, which is false in every particular.

Myself and Doc Holliday happened to go to Charleston the night that Behan went down there to subpoena Ike Clanton. We went there for the purpose to get a horse that I had had stolen from me a few days after I came to Tombstone. I had heard several times that the Clantons had it. When I got there that night I was told by a friend of mine that the man that carried the dispatch from Charleston to Ike Clanton's ranch had rode my horse. At this time I did not know where Ike Clanton's ranch was.

A short time afterwards, I was in the Huachucas locating some water rights.[14] I had started home to Tombstone. I had got within 12 or 15 miles of Charleston. I met a man by the name of McMasters. He told me if I would hurry up, I would find my horse in Charleston. I drove into Charleston and see my horse going through the streets toward the corral. I put up for the night in another corral. I went to Burnett's office to get out papers for the recovery of the horse. He was not at home, having gone down to Sonora to some coal fields that had been discovered. I telegraphed to Tombstone to James Earp and told him to have papers made out and sent to me. He went to Judge Wallace and Mr. Street. They made the papers out and sent them to Charleston by my youngest brother, Warren Earp, that night. While I was waiting for the papers, Billy Clanton found out that I was in town and went and tried to take the horse out of the corral. I told him that he could not take him out, that it was my horse. After the papers came, he gave the horse up without the papers being served, and asked me if I had any more horses to lose. I told him I would keep them in the stable after this and give him no chance to steal them.

I give here as a part of the statement a document sent me from Dodge City since my arrest on this charge which I wish attached to this statement and marked "Exhibit A." [Here counsel for prosecution objects to this paper being introduced or used for or attached as an exhibit as a part of this statement, on the ground that the paper is not on its face a statement of the defendant but a statement of other persons made long after the alleged commission of this crime. Counsel for the defense objects to any objections interpolated by counsel for the prosecution in a statutory statement made by the party charged with crime, for the reason that the law contemplates such statement shall not be interruped by the court, the counsel for the prosecution, not the counsel for the defense, or for the *farther* reason that it is perfect evidence of character lacking only the absurd? formality. Objection of counsel for prosecution overruled and the paper ordered to be filed as part of this statement.] And another document sent me from Wichita, Kansas, since this arrest, which I

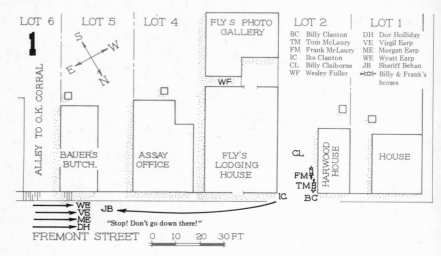

*Wyatt, Virgil, Morgan and Doc Holliday walked down Fremont
and saw the Cowboys waiting in Lot 2. They were met at Bauer's
Butcher Shop by Sheriff John Behan, who told them to not go
down there, and that he had disarmed the Cowboys.*

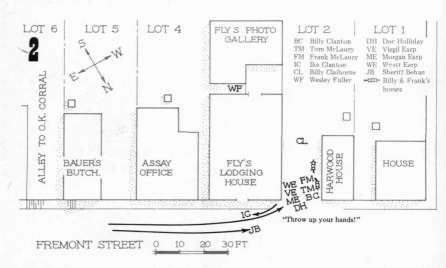

*The Earps and Holliday brushed past Behan and walked into the
fifteen foot lot where the Cowboys were waiting. Ike Clanton
darted past Wyatt saying that he was unarmed. Virgil held up his
cane in his right hand and said, "Throw up your hands!"*

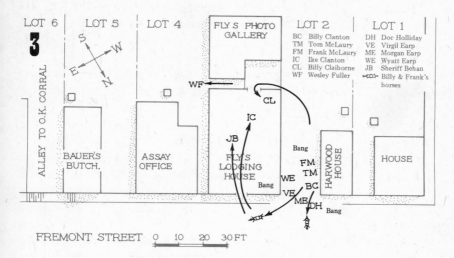

Shooting between the two groups commenced and became general. Billy Claiborne, Ike Clanton, and Johnny Behan ran to the landing behind Fly's Lodging House. The two horses bolted from the lot. Virgil, Doc and Morgan were struck by bullets.

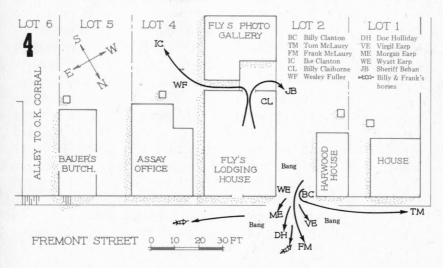

Billy Clanton feel dead at the Harwood house. Frank and Tom McLaury scrambled into the street and were hit as they returned the fire. The entire fight lasted no more than thirty seconds and history was made.

wish attached to this statement and marked "Exhibit B." [Same objection by prosecution and same ruling by the court.]

In relation to the conversation that I had with Ike Clanton, Frank McLoury and Joe Hill was four or five different times, and they were all held in the back yard of the Oriental saloon. I told Ike Clanton in one of them conversations that there were some parties here in town that was trying to give Doc Holliday the worst of it, by their talk, that there was some suspicion that he knew something about the attempted robbery and killing of Bud Philpot, and that if I could catch Leonard, Head, and Crane, I could prove to the citizens that he knew nothing of it. In following the trail of Leonard, Head, and Crane, we struck it at the scene of the attempted robbery and never lost the trail, or hardly a footprint from the time we started from Drew's ranch, on the San Pedro, until we got to Helm's ranch in the Dragoons, after following about 80 miles down the San Pedro River, and capturing one of the men, named King, that was supposed to be in with them; then across the Catalina Mountains, within 15 miles of Tucson, following their trail around the foot of the mountain, to Tres Alamos on the San Pedro River, thence to the Dragoons to Helm's ranch. They then started out from Helm's ranch. Got on their trail. They had stolen 15 or 20 head of stock, so as to cover their trail. Virgil Earp and Morgan Earp, R. H. Paul, Breakenridge the deputy sheriff, Johnny Behan the sheriff, and one or two others, still followed their trail to New Mexico. Their trails never led south from Helm's ranch, as Ike Clanton has stated. We used ever effort we could to capture those men or robbers. I was out ten days. Virgil and Morgan Earp was out 16 days, and all done all we could to catch those men; and I safely say, if it had not been for myself and Morgan Earp they would not have got King, as he started to run when we rode up to his hiding place and was making it for a big patch of brush on the river and would have got in it, if [it] had not been for us two.

[Signed]   Wyatt S. Earp

Usual sworn statement by Wells
Spicer, J.P., November 17, 1881.

Defense Exhibit "A"

To all Whom it May Concern, Greetings:

We, the undersigned citizens of Dodge City, Ford County, Kansas, and vicinity do by these presents certify that we are personally acquainted with Wyatt Earp, late of this city; that he came here in the year 1876; that during the years 1877, 1878, and 1879, he was Marshal of our city; that he left our place in the fall of 1879; that during his whole stay here he occupied a place of high social position and was regarded and looked upon as a high-minded, honorable citizen; that as Marshal of our city he was ever vigilant in the discharge of his duties, and while kind and courteous to all, he was brave, unflinching, and on all occasions proved himself the right man in the right place.

Hearing that he is now under arrest, charged with complicity in the killing of three men termed cowboys, from our knowledge of him we do not believe that he would wantonly take the life of his fellow man, and that, if he was implicated, he only took life in the discharge of his sacred trust to the people, and earnestly appeal to the Citizens of Tombstone, Arizona, to use all means to secure for him a fair and impartial trial, fully confident that when tried he will be fully vindicated and exonerated of any crime.

R. M. Wright, Representative, Ford County
Lloyd Shinn, Probate Judge, Ford County, Kansas
M. W. Sutton, County Attorney
George F. Hinkle, Sheriff, Ford County, Kansas
G. M. Homer, Chairman, County Board
J. W. Liellow, County Commissioner
F. C. Zimmerman, Treasurer and Tax Collector
G. W. Potter, County Clerk
Thomas S. Jones, Police Judge and Attorney at Law
A. B. Webster, Mayor, Dodge City, Kansas
C. M. Beeson, City Council, Dodge City, Kansas
George Emerson, City Council
P. F. Sughrue, City Council
A. H. Boyd, City Council
J. H. Philips, Dep. County Treasurer
R. G. Cook, U.S. Commissioner
Wright Beverly and Company, Merchants

The ruins of the Clanton ranch house located on the San Pedro River near Lewis Springs. (Turner Collection)

Herman F. Fringey, Postmaster, Dodge City, Kansas
O. W. Wright, Pastor, Presbyterian Church
Marsh and Son, Merchants
W. W. Robins, Groceries
H. P. Weiss, Shoemaker
Fred T. M. Wenir, Notary Public and Insurance Agent
R. C. Burns, Attorney
H. B. Bell, Dep. U. S. Marshal
T. L. McCarty, M.D.
D. E. Frost, Ex-Police Judge
Beeson and Harris, Liquor Dealers
W. F. Petillon, Register of Deeds, Ford County
J. Ormond, Bookkeeper
N. B. Klaine, Editor, (Dodge City) *Times*, City Treasurer, School
            Director, and Notary Public
Walter Straeter
J. H. Kelley, Ex-Mayor, Dodge City
Jim Anderson, Livery Man
J. McGinnis, R. R. Agent, and Agent, Wells Fargo and Co. Express
P. G. Reynolds and Son
Tom Bugg, Dep. Sheriff
Coe and Boyd, Props. Dodge House

Oscar Tsevallee, Boots and Shoes
B. C. Vanderburg, City Marshal
T. Coller, Merchant
Ed. Cooley, Constable and Dep. Sheriff
R. E. McAnulty, Cattle Dealer
Bond and Nixon, Liquor Dealers
John Mueleer, Cattle Dealer
H. F. Wray
Jno. T. Lytle, Cattle Dealer
R. W. Evans
and 13 others on paper. Notarized or acknowledged by; H. P. Myton, Clerk of the District Court, Ford County, Kansas.

[With Seal]

Defense Exhibit "B"

State of Kansas

ss

County of Sedgwick

We, the undersigned citizens of Wichita in the County and State aforesaid are well acquainted with Mr. Wyatt S. Earp and that we were intimately acquainted with him while he was on the Police force of this city, in the years A.D. 1874, 1875 and part of the year 1876. We further certify that the said Wyatt S. Earp was a good and efficient officer, and was well known for his honesty, and integrity, that his character while here was of the best, and that no fault was ever found with him as an officer, or as a man.

George E. Harris, Mayor in 1875
M. Zimmerly, Councilman in 1875
C. M. Garrison, Councilman in 1875
R. C. Ogdell, ex City Marshal
J. M. True, ex City Treasurer
Fred Sclattner, City Clerk
James Cairns, City Marshal

Sworn and subscribed to and before me this 4th day of November A.D. 1881.

Charles Hatton, Notary Public

Next Mr. Hatton adds a statement of his own:

I hereby certify that I knew personally Wyatt S. Earp during his residence in the city of Wichita. That I served four years as city attorney of said city and have known personally all of the officers of said city for the past ten years. I take great pleasure in saying that Wyatt S. Earp was one of the most efficient officers that Wichita ever had and I can safely testify that Mr. Earp is in every sense reliable and a trustworthy gentleman.

[Signed]   Charles Hatton.

HISTORICAL NOTES AND EDITORIAL COMMENTS

1. Wyatt Earp was a resident of Tombstone for about twenty-eight months.

2. Earp's law enforcement career in Tombstone was as follows: shotgun messenger for Wells Fargo for about eight months; Pima County deputy sheriff for about four months; deputy U. S. marshal almost three months; and detective for Wells Fargo for an undetermined length of time.

Wyatt also served occasionally as assistant city marshal and deputy U. S. marshal's posseman. This special work was under the direction of his brother, Virgil.

Virgil himself was Marshal of Tombstone for about five months and a deputy U. S. marshal during his whole Tombstone residence (December 1, 1879 until December 29, 1881).

3. Wyatt Earp's testimony is perhaps the most unique that was given at the Spicer Hearing. Much of it was read from a prepared document and none of it was subjected to cross-examination.

After being sworn in, Earp started his testimony in the usual verbal manner. Thomas Fitch would ask a question and Earp would give a verbal answer. Example: Q. *"What is your name and age?"* A. "My name is Wyatt Earp—32 years old last March the 19th."

This procedure continued until the fifth question was asked by the defense attorney, whereupon Earp pulled a prepared document from his pocket and started to read his testimony.

The prosecution promptly objected to the reading of testimony which allowed the introduction of evidence that might not be relevant to the current situation as verbal testimony would be. Both objections were overruled by the court (Judge Spicer), and Earp continued to read from the long document.

The fact that Wyatt Earp's testimony was not cross-examined was a distinct advantage to the defense—considerable information was introduced into the case without its contents being tested. Earp's testimony was written by Thomas Fitch, the leader of the defense team of lawyers, using source material provided by Wyatt and Virgil Earp.

4. William M. Breakenridge, Tombstone's part-time deputy, told the story of the mules on page 151 of his book, *Helldorado*:

> Several of the old-timers still living in that part of the country tell the following story regarding these mules: Curly Bill, Zwing Hunt, and Billy Grounds stole the mules and ran them down into the Sulphur Springs Valley near McLaury's ranch. At Soldiers Holes [*sic*] they sold the mules to a freighter, who hurried them back to the Chiricahua Mountains, and went to hauling saw logs for Morse's Sawmill.

The location of the McLaury Ranch at this time (1880) was not the Sulphur Springs Valley near "Soldiers Holes," but on the Babocomari River near Fairbank. The United States Census for Cochise County, 1880, lists Frank and Tom McLaury at Babocomari. The place was sometimes called the Patterson Ranch. The McLaury boys had nothing to do with the theft of the mules; but they kept them in their corral until the thieves could sell them.

First Lieutenant J. H. Hurst printed the following reward and information placard concerning the theft of the army mules from Camp Rucker in the July 30, 1880, *Epitaph*:

REWARD!!

A reward of $25 will be paid for the arrest, trial and conviction of each of the thieves who stole six (6) Government mules from Camp John A. Rucker, A.T., on the night of July 21st, 1880.

It is believed that these mules were stolen by parties known by the following names: PONY DIEHL, A. T. HANSBROUGH, MAC DEMASTERS.

It is known that the thieves were aided in the secretion of the stolen animals by parties known by the names of FRANK PATTERSON, FRANK M'LOWRY [*sic*], JIM JOHNSON, and other parties unknown.

It is known that the stolen animals were secreted at or in the vicinity of the McLowry [*sic*] Brothers ranch, on the Babacomari [*sic*] river on July 25th, 1880; and it is also believed that they were there branded on the left shoulder over the Government brand U.S., by the letter and figure D 8.

Evidence to assist in the conviction of the thieves will be furnished by the undersigned.

The present day rear entrance to the O.K. Corral.

An additonal reward of $25 will be paid for the recovery and delivery of each of these stolen animals to the undersigned.

J. H. HURST,
First Lieutenant, 12th Infantry, A. A. Q. M., Camp John Rucker, A.T.
Charleston, A.T., July 27, 1880.

Frank McLaury answered the mule theft charges with the following published in the Tombstone Weekly *Nugget*, August 5, 1880, "A Card."

On the morning of July 25th, 1880, this man Hurst came to my ranch with an escort of soldiers accompanied by several citizens [Wyatt, Virgil, and Morgan Earp], and he took me aside and told me, in substance, that he had had stolen from Camp Rucker six government mules, and stated that they were stolen by Pony Deihl, A. S. Hahsbrough and MacMasters. . .
. . . If J. H. Hurst was a gentleman, or if I could appeal to the courts for protection, I would proceed differently in this matter, but Hurst is irresponsible and I have but one course to pursue, and that is to publish to the world that J. H. Hurst, 1st. Lieut. 12th Inft., AAQM., is a coward, a vagabond, a rascal and a malicious liar. This base and unmanly action is the result of cowardice, for instead of hunting the stock himself he tried to get others to do it, and when they could not find it, in order to cover up his own wrong acts, he attempted to traduce the character and reputation of honest men.

The attitude of Frank McLaury is indeed strange. Curly Bill Brocius, Billy Grounds, and Zwing Hunt had stolen the mules from Fort Rucker, and the McLaurys and Frank Patterson had kept the animals in their pasture until they could be sold. *It is obvious who the criminals were and the list did not include Lieutenant Hurst.*

My name is well known in Arizona and thank God this is the first time in my life that the name of dishonesty was ever attached to me. Perhaps when the matter is ventilated it will be found that the Hon. Lieut. Hurst has stolen those mules and sold them, for a coward will steal, and a man who can publish the placard that bears his name is a coward. I am willing to let the people of Arizona decide who is right.

FRANK McLAURY
BABOCOMARI, AUGUST 2, 1880.

5. The McLaury boys and Frank Patterson did not take this visit by Lieutenant Hurst and his soldiers and Deputy U. S. Marshal Virgil Earp's posse lightly. Since the cowboys were nearly caught with stolen goods, they tried to lie out of it. The mules were never returned, and lasting enemies were made.

6. William M. Breakenridge, a hostile witness, again corroborated Wyatt's testimony that the Clantons and the McLaurys were friendly with the outlaws. He writes on page 105 in *Helldorado:*

The Clantons looked after the rustler's interest on the San Pedro, as a lot of stolen stock was brought from Mexico down the river, and there was no one watching the line for smugglers. The McLaurys looked after the stock brought up from Mexico through Auga Prieta, where Douglas now stands, into the Sulphur Springs Valley.

7. The Clanton gang also jumped a ranch in 1887, shortly before Ike Clanton was killed by J. V. Brighton on Eagle Creek. Isaac N. Ellinger, who owned the Cottonwood Ranch in the Animas Valley, was shot and killed by the gang.

Ike and Phineas Clanton, Lee Renfro, and Bill Jackson, the last remaining members of the gang had invited Ellinger to dinner at *Cienega Amarilla,* the Clanton Ranch. The Tombstone *Prospector,* September 14, 1887, described the "jumping" with the following words:

. . . they had but entered the room when Renfro commenced to abuse Ellinger for something about the jumping of the ranch, at the same time picking up his six-shooter from the table and walked toward Ellinger. At this junction Ike Clanton stepped between them, but Renfro suddenly threw his pistol around Ike and shot Ellinger in the breast. Mr. Ellinger lived several days in great agony, suffering a thousand deaths, and died on or about the 10th day of November last.

The Clanton gang did not profit greatly from this "jumping," because J. V. Brighton, the correspondence school detective, continued to cut down the membership. He killed Ike Clanton and Lee Renfro, and arrested

Newman Haynes Clanton (Old Man Clanton) was the head of the Clanton family.

Phineas Clanton. This left only Bill Jackson and a few other minor members of the once-powerful Clanton Gang to operate.

All of the three Clanton girls married men suspected of stealing cows.

Elizabeth Clanton	Married Pete Slaughter
Hettie Clanton	Married Charles Smith.
Mary Elsie Clanton	Married John F. Slinkard and Ebin B. Stanley.

8. This was Louis Hancock who was wounded in the jaw by John Ringo in a Safford area bar. The shooting was the result of a drunkards' quarrel. There is a marker in Tombstone's Boot Hill that states that Ringo killed Hancock in 1879, however, he is not buried there for two reasons: the shooting took place in Safford, not Tombstone; and Ringo did not kill him. A wounded man is not buried—even in Boot Hill. This is as near as Ringo ever came to a gunfight in Arizona.

9. Chief of Police Virgil W. Earp was considered to be a good officer by many of the citizens. Some believed that he would arrest his own mother if she broke the slightest law. Virgil arrested his boss, John P. Clum, for fast driving of his buggy down Allen Street; and arrested his brother Wyatt for fighting and disturbing the peace. It is certain that Ike Clanton

and Doc Holliday had respect for Virgil and stopped quarreling when he asked them to.

10. The official record of Ike Clanton's arrest by Virgil Earp on the morning of the fight is listed in the *Recorder's Docket, City of Tombstone, Book no. 1*, 1881-1886. A. O. See Chapter 1, Note 14.

11. The "buffaloeing" of Tom McLaury shortly before the fight started is an interesting study, indicating how eyewitnesses may be influenced in the description of an incident because of a partisan attitude. Bauer's testimony is of particular interest because he gave some important information concerning the clothing Earp was wearing and the gun he was carrying.

It would appear, since Wyatt Earp was Tombstone's assistant marshal at the time, that he would have taken Tom McLaury to Judge Wallace if the "cowboy" had been armed. This clash, however, may have been more personal in nature brought about by sudden anger that flared into violence when the two men accidentally bumped together on the sidewalk.

DOCUMENT NO. 94, in Justice Court, Township No. 1, Cochise County, A.T.

TERRITORY OF ARIZONA
vs.
MORGAN EARP, ET AL, DEFENDANTS,

Deposition of A. Bauer:

. . . I saw a difficulty on that day between one of the Earp brothers and Tom McLaury. [Here witness points to Wyatt Earp and says, 'That gentlemen looks like him.'] The difficulty occurred on 4th Street, I crossed Allen Street, to go to Judge Wallace's Court, Mr. Earp walked ahead of me three or four steps. I was in company with Billy Hines, the cattleman. Me and Mr. Hines both saw Tom Mclowrey [spelled in various ways in *Document no. 94]* come from Wallace's Court, and Mr. Earp was walking toward Wallace's Court, and both Mr. Earp and Mc-Lowrey walked pretty near solid together face-to-face. Mr. Hines and I stopped and looked at Mr. Earp and Tom McLowrey. They both said something one to another, which I did not understand. The moment I was willing to pass them both, to go to Wallace's Court room, Mr. Earp raised his left hand or fist-like [*sic*], and run it into Tom McLowrey's face. Tom McLowrey had both hands in his pants pockets. Mr. Earp said, 'Are you heeled or not?' 'No, I am not heeled. I have got nothing to do with anybody.' Tom McLowrey took his hands out of his pockets to ward off the striking. Tom McLowrey backed off from Mr. Earp toward the street, from the sidewalk, Mr. Earp following him, pulling a pistol with his right hand out of his coat pocket and knocked him with the pistol on his shoulder and head. McLowrey fell in about the middle of the street. He fell on his right side and raised his left hand and held it to his left ear. When I looked around a little and I saw an old gentleman have hold of Tom McLowrey, leading him along 4th Street, crossing Allen and going towards Freemont [*sic*] Street. Mr. Earp struck Tom McLowrey two or three or maybe four blows with his pistol. When Mr. Earp left Tom McLowrey lying down, he said, 'I could kill the son of a bitch!' When Tom McLowrey was struck, he opened his eyes awful large. He was dizzy and trembled.

CROSS-EXAMINATION

To queries: Wyatt Earp had on a short coat; did not have an overcoat on; it [his pistol] seemed to me an old pistol, pretty large, 14 or 16 inches long, it seemed to me.

In his cross-examination, Bauer stated that his brother had been buying cattle from the McLaurys. Since most of the residents knew, or suspected, that the McLaurys were rustlers, it is apparent that at least some of Tombstone's butchers were openly buying their beef from thieves and rustlers.

Mr. Bauer's description of Wyatt's clothing and revolver, a short time before the fight, is also significant because there is a school of historians who teach that Wyatt Earp was wearing an overcoat and carrying a highly engraved, nickel-plated revolver. The butcher distinctly said that the coat was short, and the revolver old and well-worn.

DEPOSITION OF J. H. BATCHER:

J. H. Batcher, bookkeeper for P. W. Smith, 322-28 Allen Street, Tombstone, Arizona Territory, tells of seeing Wyatt Earp strike down Tom McLowrey on 4th Street, 'between Judge Wallace's office and Allen Street. Saw Wyatt Earp about 15 feet behind. Tom McLowrey was coming down 4th Street toward Wallace's office. Wyatt Earp spoke to Tom McLowrey and said something to him, that he had never done anything against him and was a friend of his. *Tom McLowrey addressed him and said whenever he wanted to fight, he was with him* as he said that, Wyatt Earp pulled his gun and said, 'Are you heeled?'—I don't know whether he said he was or not—then Wyatt struck him, first with the palm of his hand and then hit him with his right hand with his pistol. He struck him on the side of the head. He struck him once. Tom McLowrey fell down and Wyatt Earp walked away and McLowrey got up and left.'

Whether Tom McLaury was armed or not, at this time, is of little importance (Wyatt Earp said he was). The "Cowboys" had ample opportunity to secure weapons before the Fremont Street fight. After Tom was "buffaloed" by Earp he was seen in several business establishments, including the Capitol Saloon on Fremont and Fourth Streets; and Everhardy's butcher shop opposite the Cosmopolitan Hotel on Allen Street. He could have obtained a weapon in either place. It has never been completely clear *why the "Cowboys" were talking war in their enemies' camp, and at the same time running around without weapons.*

The important thing was the demonstration of restrained power that Wyatt and Virgil used on Ike Clanton and Tom McLaury, which for all practical purposes, put them out of any possible fight that day. The blow on their heads took most of the fight out of them.

The manhandling of the two "cowboys" also demonstrated the fact that Wyatt and Virgil did not kill when alternatives, such as "buffaloeing," could be successful. *Given a chance, Wyatt and Virgil Earp would have arrested, not killed, the Clantons and the McLaurys.*

12. Most of the witnesses said Doc Holliday and Morgan Earp started the fight. For a more complete rundown of the fight, see Chapter 1, Note 17.

13. Although Wyatt said he went to work on the Wichita police force in 1874 under Marshal William (Bill) Smith, the "Proceedings of the Governing Body," *Records of the City of Wichita, Journal B*, pages 44 and 53 show that Earp was appointed to the force April 21, 1875, when Mike Meager was Marshal.

A letter Earp wrote to Lake on October 29, 1928, states the following:

Los Angeles, October 29, 1928.
Dear Mr. Lake:
I am sending today two books, also some newspaper clippings Mrs. Earp said you asked for. Mr. Cairns said that I came to Wichita in seventy-three—but it is a mistake in his part I arrived in Wichita direct from my buffalo hunt in seventy-four and not from Mo. Mr. Cairns was also wrong about my being put on the force by Mike Meager. Bill Smith was the marshal that put me on, and Meager was elected Marshal the following spring . . .

Best Wishes
Wyatt S. Earp.

One of two things is true: the records of the City of Wichita were wrong, or Wyatt's memory was failing. Under the circumstances, the latter was probably mistaken since 48 years had passed between the event and his attempt to remember it.

James Cairns, who served as a policeman with Wyatt briefly in Wichita, also failed to remember the event with complete accuracy. He remembered the marshal that had hired Wyatt, but he did not remember the right year. It is quite apparent that passing time plays havoc with an old-timer's recollections.

14. Wyatt Earp was talking about water rights that he had filed February 5, 1881, with three other men: John H. Holliday, Rich B. Clark, and James Leavy. Each claim was located on the east slope of the Huachuca Mountains. From, *Millsites No. 1*, Cochise County. Transcribed from Pima County Records.

THE
EARLY WEST

Chapter 3

VIRGIL'S TESTIMONY-
O.K. CORRAL INQUEST

Virgil Earp testified before the Spicer Hearing three days after Wyatt had read his statement. Virgil's testimony is taken from Document 94 which was transcribed by the W.P.A. At the time of the shootout, Virgil Earp was the law in Cochise County.

DEPOSITION OF MARSHAL VIRGIL W. EARP

In Justice Court, Township No. One, Cochise County, Arizona Territory

Territory of Arizona	
vs.	Deposition
Morgan Earp, et al	

On this 19th day of November, 1881, on the hearing of the above entitled cause on the examination of Wyatt Earp and J. H. Holliday, Virgil Earp, a witness of lawful age, being produced and sworn, deposes and says as follows:

Territory of Arizona	
	ss
County of Cochise	

My name is Virgil Walter Earp, I reside in Tombstone, Cochise County, Arizona. My occupation, chief of police of Tombstone and deputy United States marshal.[1]

Q. State what official position, if any, you occupied on the 25th and 26th of October last.

A. Chief of police of Tombstone and deputy United States marshal, and was acting as such on those days.

Q. State what official or other position, if any, with respect to the police department of Tombstone was occupied on the 25th and 26th of October last by Morgan Earp.

A. He was sworn in as special policeman and wore a badge with "Special Police" engraved on it, and he had been sworn and acted as special about a month.

Q. State what official or other position, if any, with respect to the police department of Tombstone was occupied on the 25th and 26th of October last by Wyatt Earp?

A. Wyatt Earp had been sworn in to act in my place while I was in Tucson, and on my return his saloon was opened and I appointed him a "special," to keep the peace, with power to make arrests, and also called on him on the 26th to assist me in disarming those parties—Ike Clanton, and Billy Clanton, Frank McLoury and Tom McLoury.[2]

Q. State what position or deputization, if any, with respect to assisting you as chief of police was occupied on the 26th of October last or at any time during the day by J. H. Holliday?

A. I called on him that day for assistance to help disarm the Clantons and McLourys.

Q. State fully all the circumstances of and attendant upon the difficulty which resulted in the death of Frank McLoury, Thomas McLoury, and Billy Clanton, commencing on the day of the difficulty and confining your answers for the present entirely to what occurred within your sight and hearing on the day of the difficulty, on the 26th of October.

A. On the morning of the 26th, somewhere about 6 or 7 o'clock, I started to go home, and Ike Clanton stopped me and wanted to know if I would carry a message from him to Doc Holliday. I asked him what it was. He said, "The damned son of a bitch has got to fight." I said, "Ike, I am an officer and I don't want to hear you talking that way, at all. I am going down home now, to go to bed. I don't want you to raise any disturbance while I am in bed."

I started to go home, and when I got ten feet away from him he said, "You won't carry the message?" I said, "No, of course I won't." I made four or five steps more. He said, "You may have to fight before you know it." [Here the counsel for the prosecution reserves the right to strike out at the close any portion of the answer.] I made no reply to him and went home and went to bed. I don't know how long I had been in bed. It must have been between 9 and 10 o'clock when one of the policemen came and told me to get up, as there was liable to be hell.

I did not get up right away, but in about half an hour I got up. I cannot tell exactly what time it was. Along about 11 or 12 I came up on the street, and met a man by the name of Lynch. I found Ike Clanton on Fourth Street between Fremont and Allen with a Winchester rifle in his hand and a six-shooter stuck down his breeches. I walked up and grabbed the rifle in my left hand. He let loose and started to draw his six-shooter. I hit him over the head with mine and knocked him to his knees and took his six-shooter from him.[3]

I asked him if he was hunting for me. He said he was, and if he had seen me a second sooner he would have killed me.

My attention was called next to them—Frank McLoury, Tom McLoury, and Billy Clanton and Ike Clanton. I arrested Ike for carrying firearms, I believe was the charge, inside the city limits. When I took him to the court room, Judge Wallace was not there. I left him in [the] charge of Special Officer Morgan Earp, while I went out to look for the Judge. And after the examination I asked him where he wanted his arms left, and he said, "Anywhere I can get them, for you hit me over the head with your six-shooter." I told him I would leave them at the Grand Hotel bar, and done so. I did not hear at that time any quarrel between Wyatt Earp and Ike Clanton. The next I saw them they were, all four—Ike Clanton, Billy Clanton, Frank McLoury, and Tom McLoury—in the gun shop of Fourth Street [Spangenberg's]. I saw Wyatt Earp shooing a horse off the sidewalk and went down and saw them all in the gun shop, filling up their belts with cartridges and looking at the pistols and guns.

There was a committee waited on me then and called me away on one side. I turned to Wyatt Earp and told him to keep peace and order till I came back and to move the crowd off the sidewalk and not let them obstruct it. When I saw them again all four of them were going in Dunbar's corral. They did not remain long there. They came out and went into the O. K. corral.[4]

I called Johnny Behan, who refused to go with me, to go to help disarm these parties. He said if he went along with me there would be a fight sure—that they would not give up their arms to me, he said, "They won't hurt me," and, "I will go down

William Milton Breakenridge, Tombstone's tax collector, jailer, and part-time lawman.

alone and see if I can disarm them." I told him that was all I wanted them to do—to lay off their arms while they were in town. Shortly after he left I was notified that they were on Fremont Street, and I called on Wyatt and Morgan Earp and Doc Holliday to go and help me disarm the Clantons and McLourys.

We started down Fourth Street to Fremont, turned down Fremont west, towards Fly's lodging house. When we got about somewheres by Bauer's Butcher Shop I saw the parties before we got there, in a vacant lot between the photograph gallery and the house west of it.[5] The parties were Ike and Billy Clanton, Tom and Frank McLoury, Johnny Behan, and the Kid.

Johnny Behan seen myself and the party coming down towards them. He left Clanton and McLoury party and came on a fast walk towards us, and once in a while he would look behind at the party he left, as though he expected danger of some kind. He met us somewhere close to the butcher shop. He threw up boths hands, like this [illustrating], and said, "For God's sake, don't go there or they will murder you."

I said, "Johnny, I am going down to disarm them." By this time I had passed him a step and heard him say, "I have disarmed them all." When he said that, I had a walking stick in my left hand and my right hand was on my six-shooter, in my waist pants [verbatim], and when he said he had disarmed them I shoved it clean around to my left hip and changed my walking stick to my right hand.[6]

As soon as Behan left them, they moved in between the two buildings, out of sight of me. We could not see them. All we could [see] was about half a horse. They were all standing in a row. Billy Clanton and Frank McLoury had their hands on their six-shooters. I don't hardly know how Ike Clanton was standing, but I think he had his hands in an attitude where I supposed he had a gun. Tom McLoury had his hand on a Winchester rifle on a horse.

As soon as I saw them I said, "Boys, throw up your hands. I want your guns," or "Arms." With that, Frank McLoury and Billy Clanton drew their six-shooters and commenced to cock them, and [I] heard them them go "click-click." Ike Clanton threw his hand in his breast, this way [shows the motion]. At that, I said, throwing both hands up, with the cane in my right hand—and said, "Hold on, I don't want that." As I said that, Billy Clanton threw his six-shooter down, full-cocked. I was standing to the left of my party, and he was standing on the right of Frank and Tom McLoury. He was not aiming at me, but his pistol was kind of past me. Two shots went off right together. Billy Clanton's was one of them. At that time I changed my cane to my left hand and went to shooting—it was general then, and everybody went to fighting. At the crack of the first two pistols the horse jumped to one side, and Tom McLoury failed to get the Winchester. He threw his hand back this way [shows the motion]. He followed the movement of the horse around, making him a kind of breastwork, and fired one if not twice over the horse's back.[7]

Court adjourned, to meet Tuesday, November 22, 1881.

EXAMINATION RESUMED. Tuesday, November 22, 1881.

Q. When you met Lynch on the morning or noon of October 26th, what did he told [verbatim] you?

Virgil Earp (1843-1905)
as he appeared as a
young man.

A. He told me to look out for Ike Clanton, that he was hunting me and allowed to kill me on sight.

Q. State what threats, if any, were made by Isaac Clanton, William Clanton, Thomas McLoury, or Frank McLoury to you or in your presence, and what threats, if any, by either of the afore-named persons were communicated to you as having been made in the presence of others, giving the name of the persons making the communications to you, in detail.

A. The first man who spoke to me about any threats was Officer Bronk. I was down home in bed when he called. He came down after [a] committment I had for a party that was in jail. It was about 9 o'clock, I should think, on the 26th of October. While he was getting the committment, he said, "You had better get up. There is liable to be hell." He said, "Ike Clanton has threatened to kill Holliday as soon as he gets up." And he said, "He's counting you fellows in, too."—meaning me and my brothers. I told him I would get up after a while and he went off.

The next man was Lynch—I've stated what he said. The next I met was Morgan and James Earp. One of them asked me if I had seen Ike Clanton. I told them I had not. One of them said, "He has got a Winchester rifle and six-shooter on and threatens to kill us on sight." I asked Morgan if he had any idea where we could find him. He said he did not. I told him then to come and go with me and we would go and arrest him and disarm him.

Several men came on Allen Street between Fourth and Fifth—miners whose names I do not know. This was after Ike Clanton's arrest and before the fight. There was one man in particular who came and said, "Ain't you liable to have trouble?" I told him I didn't know, it looks kind of that way but couldn't tell. He said, "I seen two more of them just rode in," and he said, "Ike walked up to them and was telling them about you hitting him over the head with a six-shooter." He said that one of them rode in on a horse [and] said, "Now is our time to make a fight."

This was after the arms of Ike Clanton were returned to the Grand Hotel. Just about the time the man was telling me this, Bob Hatch came and beckoned to me, as though he intended to speak to me, and said, "For God's sake, hurry down there to the gun shop, for they are all down there and Wyatt is all alone." He said, "Why they are liable to kill him before you get there." The other man told me to be careful and not turn my back on them or I would be killed, that they meant mischief, and Lynch remarked, . . .[not completed].

There was a man named W. B. Murray and a man named J. L. Fonck came at separate times and said, "I've known you are going to have trouble, and we got plenty of men and arms to assist you." Murray was the first man to approach me on the afternoon of the 26th. I was talking to Behan at the time, in Hafford's saloon, trying to get him to go down and help me disarm them. Murray took me to one side and said, "I have been looking into this matter and know you are going to have trouble. I can get twenty-five armed men at a minute's notice." He said, "If you want them, say so." I told him, as long as they stayed in the corral—the O. K. Corral—I would not go down to disarm them; if they came out on the street, I would take their arms off and arrest them. He said, "You can count on me, if there is any danger."

I walked from the corner of Fourth and Allen Streets, west, just across the street. J. L. Fonck met me there, and he said,

"The cowboys are making threats against you." and he said, "If you want any help, I can furnish ten men to assist." I told him I would not bother them as long as they were in the corral—if they showed up on the street, I would disarm them. "Why," he said, "they are all down on Fremont Street there now." Then I called on Wyatt and Morgan Earp and Doc Holliday to go with me and help disarm them.

Frank McLoury made a threat to me one day on the street. It must have been about a month before the shooting and it might have been a week after the notice in the paper [this was John P. Clum's paper, the Daily *Epitaph*] of the formation of a Vigilance Committee. Frank McLoury stepped up to me in the street between the Express Office[8] and the Grand Hotel. He said, "I understand you are raising a Vigilance Committee to hang us boys." I said, "You boys?" He said, "Yes, us and Clantons, Hicks, Ringo, and all us cowboys." I said to him, "Frank, do [you] remember the time Curly Bill killed White [first marshal of Tombstone]? "He said, "Yes." I said, "Who guarded him that night and run him to Tucson next morning, to keep the Vigilance Committee from hanging?" He said, "You boys." I said, "Who saved Johnny-behind-the-Duce from being hung?" He said, "You boys." Now do you believe we belong to it?" He said, I can't help but believe the man who told me you do." I said, "Who told you?" He said, "Johnny Behan." Now, he said, "I'll tell you, it makes no difference what I do, I will never surrender my arms to you." He said, "I'd rather die fighting than be strangled." I made some remark to him—"All right," or something—and left him.

[The counsel for prosecution moves to strike out all the preceding conversation with Frank McLoury on the grounds that it is irrelevant and contains no threats against this defendant. Taken under advisement.]

Q. State any conversation had by you, if any, with Isaac Clanton or Frank McLoury in this town with respect to obtaining information from them or either of them that should lead to the capture or killing of the parties suspected to have been engaged in the killing of Bud Philpot and the attempt to rob the Benson stage.

[Objected to by the prosecution on the grounds that the question is too broad and inquires into conversations with Frank McLoury which are more hearsay and irrelevant and for which no foundation had been laid. Objection sustained as to Frank McLoury but overruled as to Ike Clanton and admitted to contradict [*sic*] his statement.]

A. I-don't-know-what-time-it-was-but-it-was-about-3-o'clock-in-the-morning-after-the-conversation-that [This is verbatim as it appeared in the original document]. About last June, in Tombstone, Ike Clanton asked me where we could go to have a long talk, where nobody could hear us excepting those who were along at the time. We turned around the corner of Allen and Fifth Streets along side of Danner and Owen's saloon. He said, "I've had a long talk with Wyatt in regard to Leonard, Head, and Crane," and he said, "I believe I can trust you." He said, "I am going to put up a job for you boys to catch them."

I said, "How can I know you are in earnest and can trust you?" "Well," he said, "now I'll tell you all about it." He said that Leonard had a fine ranch over in the Cloverdale Country (in New Mexico). He said, "As soon as I heard of him robbing the stage I rounded up my cattle on the San Pedro here and run them over and jumped his ranch."[9] And he says, "Shortly after you boys gave up the chase, who should come riding up but Leonard, Head, and Crane." And he said, "By God, they have been stopping around there ever since and it looks as though they are going to stay." He said, "They have already told me that I would either have to buy the ranch or get off of it." He said, "I told them that I supposed, after what they had done, they would not dare to stay in the country and I supposed you would rather your friends would get your ranch than anybody else." But if they were going to stay in the country he would either get off or buy the ranch. He says, "Now you can see why I want these men either captured or killed and I would rather have them killed."

I says, "Here are three of you and there is only three of them. Why don't you capture or kill them, and I would see that you get the reward?" He says, "Jesus Christ, I wouldn't last longer than a snowball in hell if I should do that!" He says, "The rest of the gang would think we killed them for the reward and they would kill us. But," he says, "we have agreed with Wyatt to bring

John H. Behan was the first sheriff of Cochise County, Arizona, and was a constant opponent to the Earps.

them to a certain spot, where you boys can capture them." And he said, "As soon as Wyatt gets a telegram he is going to send for, in regard to the reward dead or alive, and they will give it dead or alive, we'll start right after them, to bring them over." I said, "Where will you bring them to?" He said, "Either to McLoury's ranch or Willow Springs."

"Now," he said, "I want you never to give us away or say a word about it except [to] the party you take along." There were some few more remarks made—I don't remember what they were—and we broke up for that time. This is about 3 o'clock in the morning after [the] conversation Ike Clanton had with Wyatt Earp. I had another conversation with him when he said Wyatt had showed him the dispatch saying that Wells Fargo would pay the reward dead or alive.

Q. In reference to the statements made by Isaac Clanton in his testimony, I ask you: did you ever at any time tell Isaac Clanton to tell Billy Leonard not to think that you were trying to catch him when you were running him, or to tell Billy Leonard that you had thrown Paul and the posse off Leonard's track when he left Helm's ranch at the foot of the Dragoon Mountains, or to tell Billy Leonard that you [had] taken the posse in pursuit of him on a trail in New Mexico, or to tell Billy Leonard that you had done all you could for him or to tell Billy Leonard that you wanted him to get Crane and Head and get them out of the country, because you were afraid one of them might get captured and get all his friends into trouble?

A. I never did.

Q. State now, Mr. Earp, any threats communicated to you that you have omitted to state heretofore.

A. There was a man met me on the corner of Fourth and Allen Streets about 2 o'clock in the afternoon of the day of the shooting. He said, "I just passed the O. K. Corral," and he saw four or five men all armed and heard one of them say, "Be sure to get Earp, the marshal." Another replied and said, "We will kill them all." When he met me on the corner he said, "Is your name Earp?" And I told him it was. He said, "Are you the marshal?" And I told him I was. I did not know the man. I have ascertained who he was since. His name is Sills, I believe.

Cross Examination

Q. Where does Sills live and what is his business?

A. I never met him till that day. I do not know what his business is. I don't know where he resides.

Q. At what house in Tombstone does he live?

A. I don't know, only by say-so.

Q. Can you give any information as to where he lives?

A. I understand he is stopping at the hospital.

Q. When did you last see him?

A. Yesterday. I saw him here.

Q. Who, if anybody, was present when he made that communication to you, on the corner of Fourth and Allen?

A. I don't think anybody was close enough to hear the conversation.

Q. *How long did that conversation take place before you started for Fremont Street?*

A. Somewhere in the neighborhood of a quarter or half an hour—not over half an hour—it might not have been that long.

Q. *Was it before or after Behan left Hafford's saloon?*

A. To the best of my recollection, it was just after.

Q. *At the time you took Isaac Clanton's rifle and pistol from him did you approach in the front or behind him?*

A. Behind him.

Q. *Did you speak to him before you seized his rifle?*

A. I think not.

Q. *With which hand did you take his rifle?*

A. With my left hand.

Q. *Where was your pistol when you seized his rifle?*

A. In my right hand.

Q. *In which hand was your pistol when you struck him?*

A. In my right hand.

Q. *Was he facing you or was his back towards you when you struck him?*

A. He was turned about halfway around. I don't know whether his body was turned—his head was.

Q. *Which of the Clantons or McLourys did you see putting cartridges in their belts at the gun shop on the occasion you have spoken of in your direct examination?*

A. William Clanton, Frank McLoury was standing right beside him. I don't think I saw any of the others putting cartridges in their belt. It looked like Frank McLoury was helping Billy Clanton.

Q. *Where was Tom McLoury at the time and what was he doing?*

A. I can't say. They were all in a bunch and I could not see what each was doing.

Q. *Were Isaac Clanton and Frank McLoury in the gun shop at that time?*

A. I am positive that Billy Clanton, Ike Clanton, and Frank McLoury were in there and am under the impression that Tom was there.

Q. *Where was Wyatt Earp at that time?*

A. He was standing on the edge of the sidewalk when I first discovered him in front of the gun shop.

Q. Was that during the time that Billy Clanton and the other persons you have named were in the gun shop?

A. It was. I first saw Wyatt Earp as I turned the corner of Allen and Fourth Streets, in front of the gun shop, on the edge of the sidewalk. I noticed him step into the crowd and take hold of a horse and "shoo" him off the sidewalk.

Q. What crowd do you allude [to]?

A. There was a dozen or more on the sidewalk gathered in a knot. I can't call to mind who they were.

Q. Where were Morgan Earp and Holliday at this time?

A. I don't remember seeing him [*sic*] at that time. I saw them on the corner of Allen and Fourth, about five or ten minutes before that. I can't say whether Holliday was armed at that time. Morgan Earp was.

Q. At the time spoken of, when you were in Hafford's saloon, did you have a shotgun or rifle?

A. I had a shotgun and six-shooter.

Q. When and where did you get that shotgun?

A. I-met-Robt [verbatim] got it in the Express Office of Wells Fargo, on Allen Street, at the time they were down at the gun shop. It has been at my service for six months. No one handed it to me at the time. I got it myself

Q. What did you do with it?

A. When I called Morgan Earp, Wyatt Earp, and Doc Holliday to go and help me disarm the McLourys and Clantons, Holliday had a large overcoat on, and I told him to let me have his cane and he take the shotgun—that I did not want to create any excitement going down the street with a shotgun in my hand. When we made the exchange, I said, "Come along," and we all went along.

Q. You speak of a committee that called on you when you were in front of the gun shop. Who composed that committee?

A. I don't know their names. They were miners, I should judge.

Q. At the time when Behan met you on Fremont Street and said, "For God's sake, don't go down there or they will murder you," where were Wyatt and Morgan Earp?

A. They were right behind me.

Q. Where was Holliday?

A. We were all in a bunch. I think he was also right behind me.

Q. *You say that at the commencement of the affray, two shots went off close together, and that Billy Clanton's was one of them. Who fired the other shot?*

A. Well, I am inclined to think it was Wyatt that fired it.

Q. *How many shots did you fire and at whom?*

A. I fired four shots—one at Frank McLoury and I believe the other three were at Billy Clanton. I am pretty positive one was at Frank McLoury and three at Billy Clanton.

Q. *What is Lynch's first name and place of residence?*

A. I don't know his first name. After the fight he was put on the police force.

[Signed]   V. W. Earp

Territory of Arizona | ss
County of Cochise |

I, Wells Spicer, the Justice of the Peace before whom the foregoing examination is being held do hereby certify that the foregoing deposition was taken and reduced to writing by F. W. Craig, under my direction, and was then read over to him and he declared the same to be correct and signed the same as his deposition in my presence.

Given under my hand this 23rd day of November, 1881.

Wells Spicer,
Justice of the Peace

HISTORICAL NOTES AND EDITORIAL COMMENTS

1. This statement indicates that Virgil was the 1881 police power in the City of Tombstone, as well as the whole county. Virgil Earp, as a Deputy U. S. Marshal, led posses hunting for the Benson and Bisbee stage robbers. As Chief of Police in Tombstone he led a posse to the Harwood vacant lot and attempted to arrest the Clantons and McLaurys.

Before coming to Tombstone in late 1879, Virgil Earp had held a number of law enforcement positions in Prescott, Arizona. [See, *Oaths and Bonds Records*, Yavapai County Courthouse, Prescott, Arizona.] At various times Virgil was night watchman, constable, Deputy Sheriff, and Deputy United States Marshal.

Following his Tombstone tenure, he was elected the first City Marshal of Colton, California; and during the year that he died, 1905, he was a deputy sheriff for Esmeralda County, Nevada.

One of the highlights of Virgil W. Earp's law enforcement career came in 1900 in Prescott, Arizona, where he was nominated for sheriff by acclamation by the Republican Convention of Yavapai County. [See, The *Arizona Republican*, Wednesday morning, September 26, 1900:]

VIRGIL EARP'S RECORD

The Kind of a Man Yavapai Republicans Want for Sheriff.

Virgil Earp was nominated for sheriff by acclamation, by the Republican Convention at Prescott last Saturday. At the ratification meeting held in the evening by the McKinley-Roosevelt Club, candidates were present and expressed themselves.

Earp was called upon and made one of the best speeches of the evening. "No doubt," he said, "many of you have heard of me. I want to tell you a few things. In 1874 I went to Dodge City, and I tell you boys, she was the wildest town on the American Continent. I had been there only a short time when business men and property owners came to me and said, 'Earp, you must help us to overcome the lawlessness in this city.' I replied, 'I don't want it, give it to someone else.' They said, 'If you don't take the city marshalship we will have to leave town.' So in the interest of law and order I accepted, and I leave it to the law-abiding citizens of Dodge City as to whether I performed my duty or not. [Editor's note: No contemporary records have been found that indicates that Virgil was an officer in Dodge City at any time.]

"The year 1876 saw me in Prescott. On my arrival I soon found out that some of the boys whom I had driven out of Dodge City were there. As soon as they saw me they concluded that if they were going to make any gunplay or shoot up the town they had better do it before I became identified with the country, so they started in at once to shoot up the town and defy the authorities of Prescott. Ed Rowen was sheriff. Do you remember that time, Eddie?" said Earp, addressing Judge E. W. Wells, who was in the chair.

"I do, well, Virgil!" responded the Judge.

"Well," continued Earp, "Rowen asked me to go. 'I am a new-comer; get someone else.' But he insisted. Whether I performed my duty then you ask Judge Wells and others. [Virgil was referring to the taking of two badmen that he helped the Sheriff and a small posse kill.]

"A few years later I was in Tombstone, and I tell you, gentlemen and ladies, she was a hot town. I had been there a short time when such men as E. B. Gauge came to me. They said, 'Virgil, you must be City Marshal and clean up this town of its disorderly and lawless elements.' I said: 'I don't want it: get someone else.' They replied, 'If you don't, we'll have to shut down our mines.' So I accepted. Fellow citizens, let E. B. Gauge answer, and he will tell you whether I performed my duty and whether I stood for the protection of life and property and the enforcement of law. Let Wells Fargo answer also. [Wells, Fargo & Company gave Virgil a gold-plated star for outstanding service to the express company.] Well, I moved to Yavapai County and have been leading a quiet life for years. [He was living on a small ranch near Kirkland, Arizona.] I came up here to the Republican Convention. Republicans, Judge Wells, and others came to me and said: 'Earp, we want you to accept the nomination for sheriff.' As at Dodge City and Tombstone, I answered, 'I don't want it, give it to someone else,' and the Republicans said, 'No one will have it.' So I was nominated, and if elected you can count on it that I will, as in former years, stand for good government and the protection of property."

Mr. Gauge was asked about Earp, and he said, "I know personally that whatever Virgil Earp did in Tombstone was at the request of the best men in Cochise County and I wish to remark that if Earp is elected sheriff of Yavapai County, all classes and all interests, individual and corporate, will receive fair and just treatment at his hands."

Virgil W. Earp was not destined to be Sheriff of Yavapai County, however. Because of failing health, he dropped out of the race.

2. Proper names are often misspelled in Document no. 94. The name of the McLaury brothers is variously spelled McLoury, McLowrie, McLowrey, and McLowry, etc. Fremont Street, named for General John C. Fremont of Civil War and western exploration fame, is often misspelled Freemont. Many other proper names are often misspelled. Mr. Hayhurst, the copyist and original editor for the Works Project Administration (WPA) was so upset with the spelling in one short paragraph where William Claiborne's name was spelled *Claborn*, and then *Clayborn* in the next line, that he noted, "If the testimony is as flexible and careless as the spelling of proper names, there is little wonder that the issue involved has remained unsettled for more than 50 years."

It is the opinion of this editor, however, that while the spelling is indeed atrocious, this is a less objectionable condition than Mr. Hayhurst's partisan treatment of the material. Mr. Hayhurst's footnotes reveal a bias *for* the "rustlers" and *against* the Earps which is much more distracting than the poor spelling.

3. The arrest of Ike Clanton by City Marshal Earp raised the ire of the "cowboy" faction to a high level. Marshal Earp, it seems, approached Clanton from behind and quickly "buffaloed" him without warning. Earp felt that this quick maneuver was necessary to prevent Clanton from killing him, the arresting officer, or hurting some innocent citizen on the street with a stray bullet.

Ike had been roaming the streets for hours, threatening to kill the Marshal and his deputies, and was illegally armed to accomplish this threat. According to A. W. Bork and Glenn G. Boyer, "The O. K. Corral Fight at Tombstone, a Footnote by Kate Elder," *Arizona and the West*, p. 79:

> When Holliday and the Earps appeared on the streets, he [Clanton] repeatedly cried, "the ball will open."
> He had also paid an early morning visit to Fly's Rooming house hunting Doc Holliday with a rifle and a six-shooter.

In spite of these overt threats, the "cowboy" faction wanted Virgil Earp to handle Ike Clanton with kid gloves. A number of other people wondered what Ike had done to deserve any consideration at all.

See Chapter 1, Note 14, for the official report of the arrest of Ike Clanton.

4. The "cowboys" did not stop long in the O. K. Corral, but moved on to the Harwood vacant lot next to Fly's building. Some believe they were here waiting for Doc Holliday to come back to his room, so they could "do him in."

5. The actual location where the fight started was the northeast part of lot no. 2, block no. 17. The closest part of the O. K. Corral was ninety feet from this spot. The fight was not in the O. K. Corral.

6. The fact that Chief of Police Virgil W. Earp was carrying a walking stick (cane) in his right hand supports his assertion that he did not expect trouble, and that he intended to arrest, not kill, the Clantons and McLaurys. A cane is a strange weapon indeed for a man to carry in his gun-hand, if he is bent on murder.

Much has been written about the shotgun that Virgil gave to Doc Holliday, on Fourth Street, shortly before the fight. In actual fact, it could have been long or short barreled, 10 or 12 gauge—Wells Fargo used them all. It was general practice to use 10 gauge guns on the coaches, and 12 gauge for guard duty in the towns.

7. Many persons, especially "cowboy" sympathizers, have insisted that Tom McLaury and Ike Clanton were not armed at the time of the fight. If they were not armed, it was their own fault, since they had ample opportunity to replace weapons confiscated by the police. (Only Ike Clanton had weapons taken by the police and they were placed in the Grand Hotel.) Ra-

tional thinking men would not tarry in the enemy territory, talking war, and not be armed.

It was generally acknowledged by the "cowboy" crowd that Billy Clanton and Frank McLaury were armed, and were wearing belts and holsters. The "cowboy" supporters had to acknowledge the fact that some of the "cowboys" were armed, or how else could Virgil and Morgan Earp, and Doc Holliday, be hit by pistol fire? The same group, however, declared that Ike Clanton, Tom McLaury, William Claiborne, and Wesley Fuller—Clanton allies all—were unarmed. One would wonder what they intended to do at a gunfight without a weapon.

It makes no difference whether they were armed or not, and who fired the first shot is unimportant. A person in the company of armed and defiant men, in this case Frank McLaury and Billy Clanton, is an accessory and subject to same violence as his armed companions.

There are a number of options to consider as to why the "Cowboys" were in the Harwood vacant lot (Lot no. 2, Block no. 17) and what they intended to do:

a. If they were leaving town as several of them had said, why would they leave their weapons behind them in town? It was not against the law to wear, or carry, weapons when you were leaving town.

If the "cowboys" were leaving town their team and wagon would have been hitched up.

b. Ike Clanton and Tom McLaury may have had all of the fight knocked out of them by the "buffaloeing" so thoroughly administered by Wyatt and Virgil Earp. They may have decided to go home and return later for their arms. The fight with the Earps would be continued later, and under more favorable conditions.

The "cowboys," Billy Claiborne and Wes Fuller, had not come to the vacant lot to fight, but only to see their friends off to their various ranches.

c. The "cowboys" had assembled in the vacant lot to wait for Doc Holliday to return to his room. (He lived at Fly's Rooming House), as they wanted to "do him in." Perhaps they wanted to beat up Doc and humiliate him; but more likely, they would have killed him and left the country (go to New Mexico and raise sheep).

Their plan for revenge was spoiled by the arrival of Sheriff John H. Behan on the scene, who was followed shortly by the Earp posse.

d. Ike Clanton and Tom McLaury were depending on arming themselves with the rifles in the scabbards on the horses in case the Earps would appear before they left town. This was not a practical plan however, since the two horses with the "cowboy" party belonged to Billy Clanton and Frank McLaury who had just reached town and had not yet stabled their mounts. Ike Clanton and Tom McLaury did not have horses in town, since they had come to town on the 25th in a spring wagon.

It can readily be seen that the horse had accidentally stopped in front of Tom McLaury, when he apparently made a try to pull the rifle from the scabbard.

e. The "cowboys" were all armed and ready for a fight. Their only problem was they were not quick enough in getting their weapons and going to work.

The remains of the McLaurys and Billy Clanton,
victims of the O. K. Corral fight.

Sheriff Behan, or other spectators, picked up the pistols dropped by Ike Clanton and Tom McLaury, etc.

f. The "cowboys" were all talk, just blowing off steam. Although they had berated the Earps for 24 hours, they had no idea that a shooting would develop. This confidence resulted in the "cowboys" being caught off-guard when the Earps did appear.

When Doc Holliday and Morgan Earp opened the fight by beating Frank McLaury and Billy Clanton to the draw, the remaining "cowboys" were completely undone, either fleeing the fight or failing to go into action quickly enough.

We only have the word of Sheriff John H. Behan that Ike Clanton, Tom McLaury, Billy Claiborne, and Wesley Fuller were not armed—that is, other than the conflicting testimony of the survivors of the fight. Sheriff Behan, himself, admitted that he had not searched Tom McLaury very carefully, and that he might have had a pistol in his waistband (under his long blouse).

As Judge Wells Spicer said in his decision at the conclusion of the Spicer Hearing:

The supposed graves of the cowboys who were slain on October 26, 1881. Although the headboards say they were murdered, the Earps were exonerated of this charge. (Turner Collection).

There is a dispute as to whether Thomas McLowery was armed at all, excepting with a Winchester rifle that was on the horse beside him. I will not consider this question because it is not of controlling importance. Certain it is that the Clantons and McLowerys had among them at least two six-shooters in their hands and two Winchester rifles on their horses. Therefore, if Thomas McLowery was one of a party who were thus armed and were making felonious resistance to an arrest, and in the melee that followed was shot, the fact of his being unarmed, if it be a fact, could not of itself criminate the defendants, if they were not otherwise criminated.

8. Here we have a contemporary account of the location of the Wells, Fargo Express Company's office in November, 1881. "Frank McLoury stepped up to me in the street between the Express office and the Grand Hotel," said Virgil Earp. The Grand Hotel stood at 424 Allen Street, on the south side of the street. The Express Company was located at 427 Allen Street, on the north side, a few doors east of Haffords Corner.

9. For details of ranch "jumping," see Chapter 2, Note 7.

Chapter 4

JAMES TALKS

An interview given by James Earp to the Los Angeles DAILY TIMES was published March 28, 1882, a week after Morgan was buried in Colton, California.

JAMES C. EARP RECOUNTS THE HISTORY OF THE BITTER FEUD WITH THE COWBOYS

Visits Los Angeles——Who He Is and a Bit of Family History—— "Jumping from a Coal Pit into a Parlor."

Yesterday James C. Earp and wife, of Tombstone, Arizona, registered at the Pico House, and in the afternoon Mr. Earp allowed a *Times* reporter a lengthy interview. He stated that he had just come from Colton, where he had been visiting his parents, and had buried his brother, Morgan, a week ago last Sunday. He had left Tombstone a few days previous in company with his [wife] and Morgan's wife, bringing his brother's dead body to Colton for burial. Mrs. Morgan Earp is now with her parents-in-law at Colton. Mr. Earp is accompanied here by his wife, a very beautiful brunette. He himself is a blond, with blue eyes, light hair, about five feet six inches high, rather stout of build, has a heavy mustache, and very neatly dressed.
WHAT TO SAY
At the outset of the interview he said that whatever he would say might be used for publication. The Earp family originally came from Kentucky, and consisted at present of the two parents, the five famous brothers of Tombstone, and a half brother,[1] by their father's first wife, who is living in Kansas.

The boys were all born in Illinois,[2] and lived during their youth in Iowa. They afterwards moved into Kansas, and about three years ago the five boys

WENT TO TOMBSTONE,[3]

When there were but a half dozen houses in the place, the parents coming to Colton. At Tombstone they have by hard work and close attention to business acquired many thousand dollars worth of property,[4] having one claim next to the Bizner mine, for which they refused an offer of $16,000. They also own twenty acres of choice agricultural land adjoining the town site of Tombstone. Their industry and perseverance won them the honor of being elected to various offices of trust, Virgil Earp being United States Marshal. Wyatt Earp is United States Deputy Marshal and Morgan Earp was selected by Wells, Fargo & Company as their messenger.[5] It was the performance of their duties as officers that

THE FIRST TROUBLES AROSE

About a year ago the Bisbee stage was robbed of a vast amount of treasure and the United States mail.[6] The Earp boys at once proceeded to work up the case, and soon found that two fellows named Peter Spence and Frank Stilwell were implicated. These parties they promptly arrested. Their preliminary examination was held at Tucson. Spence was cleared and Stilwell was bound over till the next term of court, which is now about to assemble. [Stilwell was killed a few days ago.] Stilwell, after getting out on bail, commenced stirring up bad blood in Tombstone. Associated with him were Frank and Tom McLowery, Billy and Ike Clanton, John Ringo and Peter Spence. These all

BEGAN MAKING THREATS

Against the Earp boys, who were informed by friends of their danger, and prepared themselves for self-defense, not knowing at what moment they might be shot down underhandedly by the villains against whom they had only done their simple duty in enforcing the law. In the language of Mr. Earp, "They all made an agreement that they had to get rid of the Earp boys before they could do anything in that country." The state of affairs became worse, and threats became more frequent, meddlesome busybodies carried tales and made affairs worse. At last Frank McLowery came to the Earp boys and said, "I understand you have

Wyatt Earp was born in this house in Monmouth, Illinois. (Turner Collection).

JOINED THE VIGILANCE

Committee to hang us fellows." To which Virgil Earp promptly replied, "Frank, you know that ain't so. I want to know what your authority is? You know that anybody that told you that is a liar!" Frank replied, "Well, I heard so, but if you say it ain't so, I will believe you." They then asked who told him, and he replied, "Johnny Behan." The Earps then replied that Johnny Behan was a condemned misrepresenting _____ _____. To which Frank answered, "Well, Virgil, I believe you." Nothing more was said until the

DIFFICULTY WITH IKE CLANTON

About five or six months ago, about the 25th or 26th of last October, Ike Clanton came into Tombstone, and "got on a tear," and said he was going to kill the Earps on sight. James heard of it and told Virgil about Ike's threats. They then went to look for Ike, and found him near the Post Office on Fourth Street. Virgil walked up to him, and said "Ike, I want your gun."[7] Clanton turned around, and threw his Winchester rifle down on Virgil Earp, who being close at hand, caught the gun and threw it over to one side, and drawing his six-shooter knocked Clanton down with it, and then arrested him, and took him before Judge Wells [Spicer] and he was fined for carrying concealed weapons. Ike then sent for his brothers to come to town, who, when they did, got their guns, swearing they would

KILL THE EARPS

On sight. Different citizens came and told Virgil Earp that four or five armed men declaring their intentions to kill him were in town. They wanted him to go and disarm these men. Virgil then called upon his brothers Wyatt and Morgan, and Doc Holliday, to go with him and disarm the cowboys.

The Clanton party were back of the O. K. Corral on Fremont Street and thither Marshal Earp and his posse were going, on their way to do their legal duty. When pretty near there they met Sheriff Behan coming back, who said to the Earps, "Boys, don't go down there; you'll get murdered." Virgil replied, "I have to go and do my duty and disarm them."

Behan then came on a little further and met Morgan and Wyatt Earp and told them that he had disarmed the Clanton crowd.

The Earp party then went on till they were about ten feet from the Clantons, when Virgil said, "Boys, throw up your hands. Give up your guns." The Clantons replied, "All right," and commenced drawing their pistols and shooting.[8] The Earps replied likewise. Billy Clanton and Frank and Tom McLowery were killed instantly. Ike broke and run, and left his dead brother on the field. Morgan Earp was shot through the shoulder. Virgil Earp was shot through the leg. This fight occurred about three o'clock in the afternoon. James Earp was just sitting down to supper in his house about a hundred and fifty yards from the fighting. At the first shot he grasped his pistol and rushed to the scene, and got there in time to see Tom McLowery go down in death. Doc Holliday and Wyatt Earp were arrested and cleared in the preliminary examination. The grand jury also

REFUSED TO INDICT THEM

Last January a desperate attempt was made to take Virgil Earp's life. It is not known who did it.[9] He was coming out of the Oriental Saloon to go home, when three double-barrelled shotguns, filled with buckshot, were fired at him. Two of the shots struck his back and were cut out afterwards. His left arm was badly shattered, the humerus bone being broken. The surgeons afterwards took out some six inches of it, thus rendering

James Cooksey Earp, oldest of the five Earp brothers.

the arm perfectly useless. Virgil is now at Colton, and yet suffers from his wounds, but is slowly recovering.

KILLING OF MORGAN EARP

This took place on the 18th inst. The Earp brothers had been to hear the Lingard troupe. On coming away, friends told them to be on the lookout. They went into a saloon, and Morgan Earp with Bob Hatch and the proprietor and several others commenced playing pool. Morgan went around to the end of the billiard table, and turning his back to a glass door, bent down to play, when the

FATAL SHOTS WERE FIRED

From the outside. One struck him in the back and came out through the stomach. Another hit his spine, [10] and going through him, struck another man in the leg. They carried Morgan into an-

Morgan S. Earp, born April 24, 1851, and murdered on March 18, 1882, while playing pool at Campbell and Hatch's Saloon in Tombstone.

other room and he lived just an hour. Charlie_____ spoke to him and said, "Morgan, do you know me?" He answered, "This is a hard way to die." He then said to an old chum, "Tip, old boy, I have played my last game of pool." His body was brought to Colton and buried.

The murderers of Morgan Earp were discovered by the confession of Peter Spence's wife, who implicated Spence, Stilwell, some Mexicans, and others.[11] Mr. Earp admitted that his crowd had found partial revenge in their deaths, and would seek more.

PRESENT MOVEMENTS

The papers stated the Earps refused to be arrested a few days ago. Mr. Earp said this was not so. The truth of it was that Sheriff Behan or Paul had never said anything about warrants or arrests. Behan said to them, "I want to see you." Wyatt replied,

"Behan, I don't want to see you; I have seen you once too often."
Afterwards he said, "I will see Paul at Tucson." Mr. Earp here
further said his brothers had no idea of taking to the Dragoon
Mountains, nor had they been there.[12] They were at Sycamore
Springs, about six miles from Tombstone. They had too much
property in Tombstone to leave it, and they propose to stay
there and fight it out to the bitter end. This is his

FIRST TRIP TO LOS ANGELES

He said it was "like jumping from a coal pit into a parlor," to come up here from Tombstone; the only thing that kept
him there was his mines; every kind of business is overdone; will
probably go back to Colton today; and will return to Arizona as
soon as he hears from his brothers, doesn't know anything about
their subsequent movements since his leaving the territory, only
what he has seen in the papers; he is forty-two years old, and the
eldest of the five brothers; Tombstone has between four and
five thousand inhabitants; business is dull, and lots of men are
idle.[13]

HISTORICAL NOTES AND EDITORIAL COMMENTS

1. The half brother was Newton Jasper Earp, born of Nicholas
Porter Earp and his first wife, Abigail Storm Earp, on October 7, 1837, in
Kentucky.

2. James Earp is wrong here because he and two of his brothers,
Virgil and Newton, were born in Kentucky.

3. The Earps lived in Tombstone for about 28 months.

4. A partial list of mining claims that were recorded in the Earp
name, in the Tombstone Mining District, reads as follows:

DATE	LOCATORS	NAME OF CLAIM
12-6-1879	V.W., W.S., J.C. Earp & Robert Winders	1st North Ext. Mtn. Maid

12-10-1879	Same as above	Earp
1-14-1880	Same as above and A.S. Neff.	Grasshopper
2-8-1880	V.W., W.S., J.C. Earp	Dodge
2-16-1880	Same as above	Mattie Blaylock
2-16-1880	Wyatt Earp & A. S. Neff	Comstock
2-21-1880	W.S., V.W., J.C. Earp & A. S. Neff.	Rocky Ridge
4-20-1880	Wyatt Earp	Long Branch
11-4-1880	C. Billicke, W. Earp, Albert Steinfield	Ole Bull
date unknown	Virgil Earp	Red Star

For the records of these mines, see *Transcribed* Records of Mines, Cochise County.

The Earps also filed extensive water rights in the Huachuca Mountains on February 3, 1881. For these records, see *Millsites*, Book No. 1, Cochise County.

In addition to the above listed holdings, the Earps and their associates held many lots in the town itself. Examples of these holdings, as indicated by the 1881 tax rolls for Tombstone, are as follows:

PROPERTY (BLOCK)	LOT (NUMBER)	TAXPAYER
29	22	Earp bros. & Winders
V	3 lots	Earp, James
29	23	Earp, V.W. & W.S.
29	24	Earp, James
29	1	Winders, R.J. & Earp, V. W.
29	2	Earp, W.S. & J.C.
M	1	Winders, R.J. Earp, V.w
M	2	Winders, R.J., Earp, V.W.
M	3	Earp, James
M	4	Earp, Wyatt

For some unknown reason, four of the Earp mining claims were taxed in 1881 by the City of Tombstone: The First North Extension of the Mountain Maid, the Grasshopper, Mattie Blaylock, and the Longbranch. Only a small part of one of them, the First North Extension, actually lay inside the city limits.

There is a sizable group of historians who question the Earps financial ability to purchase the above listed town lots, saying that the "Earps must have been robbing stages," in order to have this much money; but in truth, most of their town property was located on the First North Extension of the Mountain Maid, a mining claim that extended into the west end of the Tombstone town site. They obtained this property for the fee of recording a mining claim.

The Earps were not poor, as one writer of western Americana contended when he described how the Earp women took in washing and ironing to feed the indolent men. This is untrue since as early as August 27, 1880, the Earp brothers leased two of their mining claims, the Comstock and the Grasshopper, to R. F. Pixley, a San Francisco investor, for a total of $6,000, which was a handsome sum in 1880. For information about these leases, see *Bonds*, Book 1, Cochise County, *TRANSCRIBED* from Pima County records.

The above listed real eastate holdings, plus numerous leases, mortgages, and other business transactions, clearly point to the fact that they were businessmen, not fly-by-night desperadoes as depicted by many writers.They were in Tombstone to make money, and remain there as permanent residents.

5. No Earp ever held an elective office in Tombstone; although Virgil had been elected Constable at Prescott, Arizona, and in 1887 he was elected as the first Marshal of the newly incorporated city of Colton California.

No actual results of the election for constable of the Prescott Precinct was found by the author, but the results of the vote is located in *Book Bonds*, pp. 60 and 61 in the records of Yavapai County, where the bond and oath of V. W. Earp is recorded:

" . . . . whereas the above bonded V. W. Earp was on the 5th day of November, 1878 elected to the office of constable in and for Prescott Precinct in the county of Yavapai."

As far as the election for city marshal in Colton was concerned, a much more complete record exists. *Book "E" Minutes of Supervisors*, San Bernardino County, pp. 80 and 81, as well as the *Minutes of the Common Council*, Book 1, City of Colton, recorded the results of the voting:

FOR CITY MARSHAL

Candidate	Votes
V. W. Earp	109
William Brown	61
L. S. Abel	1

Wyatt Earp was elected to the office of constable in the township of Larmar, Missouri, on November 17, 1870. Although an extensive newspaper campaign was conducted by the candidates for the office, Wyatt's name was not mentioned as being among the job seekers. He, evidently, was elected by a "word of mouth" write-in campaign. In any case, the *South-West Missourian* of November 17, 1870, gives the following results:

ELECTION RESULTS

For Justice of the Peace, in Lamar Township,

G. W. Shawen	145
Sam Bowman	136
N. P. Earp	135
M. Pyle	116
A. McAllister	21

For Constable, Lamar Township,

Wyatt Earp	137
N. J. Earp	108
B. Yard	41
Josiah Hartman	2

It was a heated campaign, with the principal issue being whether or not hogs should be allowed to run loose on the streets.

In spite of the fact that many historians have believed that Wyatt Earp was Lamar's first constable, this may not be true. Five months before the election of November 17, 1870, an unidentified "Constable Earp" was patrolling the town's streets, as this humorous *South-West Missourian* article of June 16, 1870, states:

COME TO GRIEF

One of our citizens had a brother from a distance call to see him on Monday last, and having not seen each other for a long time, they started around town to have a good time, generally. Taking aboard a good supply of "forty rod," they wandered around town until evening when Constable Earp found one of them upon the street incapable of taking care of himself and took him down to a stone building which he has appropriated for use of just such customers. As Mr. Earp was about turning the key upon his bird, the other came staggering up enquiring for his brother. Mr. Earp opened the door and slid him in. Coming up to the square, Mr. Earp met another hard case in the shape of a tramping butcher, who asked Mr. Earp to purchase him a pencil in place of one he alleged Mr. Earp had borrowed of him some time previous. Mr. Earp enticed him down to the stone building to procure him a pencil, and of course he shared the fate of the other two. There being a hole in the roof of the building the three caged birds managed to crawl out before morning, and the stranger not liking the reception he met with here, left for parts unknown. The other two were brought before Esq. Earp, [probably N. P. Earp, a Justice of the Peace] and fined $5 and costs, each. A few more examples, and the town will be the better for it.

6. The Bisbee stage robbery took place on the night of September 8, 1881, and Frank Stilwell, Behan's deputy, and Peter Spencer were arrested by a posse made up of Wyatt and Morgan Earp, Marshall Williams, and Deputy Sheriff Breakenridge.

The *Epitaph*, three days after the robbery, stated that the two suspected highwaymen were examined before Wells Spicer, a justice of the peace in Tombstone, and admitted to bail in the sum of $7,000 each— $5,000 for robbing Wells, Fargo & Company and the U. S. Mail, and $2,000 for robbing D. B. Bea of $600.

The actual trial started on October 21, 1881, in Tucson and was reported in the October 24, 1881, issue of the *Epitaph*:

*John P. Clum,
a close friend
to the Earps
and the former
editor of
Tombstone's
EPITAPH.
Clum died on
May 2, 1932.*

THE BISBEE STAGE ROBBERY

The Trial at Tucson ——— Graphic Story of the Driver

Journal, October 21

Yesterday morning at 10 o'clock the preliminary hearing was convened before Commissioner Stiles, of Pete Spence and Frank Stilwell, charged with robbing the mails carried on the stage running between Tombstone and Bisbee on the night of September 8th. Throughout the day a larger crowd of listeners occupied the benches in the County Court room, and a great deal of interest was manifested in the testimony. United States District Attorney Pomroy, assisted by Judge Campbell and Mr. Savage of Bisbee, are attorneys for the prosecution, and Morgan and Zabriskie for the defense.

There were eight witnesses examined for the prosecution yesterday, and there will be probably as many more produced by that side before the close of the case. The defense will also place upon the stand a goodly number. Thus apparently the trial will last at least a couple of days longer although the business is being pushed as fast as justifiable.

It being impossible to publish all the testimony adduced, only the story of the stage driver is given.

Levi McDaniels stated: My age is 41, reside at Bisbee; drive stage by occupation; on night of September 8th do not recollect where I was; about that time was driving stage from Tombstone to Bisbee; I was robbed about three miles the other side of Hereford; the first I knew the lead horses jumped out of the road to the right and somebody said "hold on;" I saw a man standing near my rear leader, with a double barreled shot-gun; Looking to the right, saw another man with a six-shooter walking toward me; it was near 11 o'clock; the man with the six-shooter walked up to me and said, "Boys, don't shoot there's no need of it." He stepped two or three steps towards me and told me to throw out the mail sack; I did so; the same man then said, "throw out everything on this boot;" I threw out everything excepting a bundle of blankets, which he said he did not want; he then told the passengers to get out on the opposite side of the coach from him and hold up their hands; he walked around and commenced robbing them; saw him rob two or three; think I had five passengers; he then told me to drive on; I started when the man with the shot-gun said, "Hold on there," and to the man with the six-shooter said, "Look on top;" he then stepped upon the boot of the coach and went through the man sitting by me, saying as he came up, "Maybe you have got some sugar;" he then went through his pockets; he then got down and told me to drive on; the passengers went along; I did not leave my seat during the robbery; the man with the shot-gun pointed at me; the men were disguised with handkerchiefs tied just below the eyes, and hats turned down; they were roughly dressed; one was a pretty large man, the other not so large.

EPITAPH, October 24, 1881

The Stage Robbery Trial

Journal, 22nd

The hearing in the case of the Bisbee stage robbers Stilwell and Spence, was continued yesterday before United States Commissioner Stiles. The court room, as upon the day previous, was filled with spectators.

The principal witness was John Hiles, of Bisbee, who testified to overhearing a private conversation between the two prisoners in Bisbee, in which Stilwell said: "we are suspected of this stage robbery, and we must put this money away, for I expect we will be arrested." Spence said: "Let's let John——meaning me——know about this, and we can have him for a witness." Stilwell said, "it is not necessary to let him know anything about it." The witness then passed out of hearing, not thinking it necessary to hear any more. Hiles also testified as to the identity of the tracks made in the mud near where the stage was overhauled. He was previous to that time in the employ of one of the defendants, and there had been unsatisfactory financial transactions between them.

R. P. Dever, of Bisbee, a shoemaker, testified to removing the heels from a pair of boots belonging to Stilwell, and replacing them with others, much broader. This occurred after the robbery.

D. W. Weldt, a Bisbee butcher, gave testimony as an expert in identifying the tracks of men and animals.

The search for the rest of the gang of Bisbee stage robbers went on after the acquital of Pete Spence, and the death of Frank Stilwell. Finally, nearly five months later important arrests were made in Texas, and on February 14, 1882, the following item appeared in the *Nugget.*

FOR STAGE ROBBERY

Parties Charged with Robbing the Bisbee Stage Arrested in Texas

Warrants were issued yesterday from Justice Spicer's court upon complaint of Charles A. Bartholomew [shotgun messenger on Bisbee Coach], for the arrest of Pony Dehl, Al Tiebot, and Charles Haws, charged with robbing the Bisbee stage containing treasure in charge of Wells, Fargo & Co. amounting to $6,500 [actually $2,500]. The parties referred to are at present in Cisco, Texas, where they are under arrest awaiting the arrival of an officer to bring them here for trial. They are also charged with robbing the U. S. Mail, for which crime they will be examined before the U. S. Commissioner.

The gang of highwaymen were all gathered in by the long arm of the law, and brought before the bar of justice; but not one of them paid the price for his crime.

7. Virgil Earp actually slipped up behind the armed Ike Clanton and struck him on the head with his pistol. This was the only prudent way for a policeman to handle an armed and dangerous drunk. (See Chapter 1, Note 14).

8. Doc Holliday and Morgan Earp started the fight by firing the first two shots. Judge Spicer, himself, admitted in his decision that followed the hearing that the Earp side fired first. (See Chapter 1, Note 17).

9. Wyatt Earp and numerous other persons knew who had attempted to kill Virgil Earp on the night of December 28, 1881. In an undated letter, Wyatt Earp to Stuart N. Lake, we find the following:

. . . . Here is an answer to your questions. Virgil saw Stilwell go into the vacant building just as he was coming out of the Oriental. After going his rounds before going home. We found Ike Clanton's hat, that he dropped in getting away from the rear end of the building.

10. Only one of the two shots fired struck Morgan Earp. See, *County of Cochise, Inquest on Morgan Earp*, No. 68, Testimony of Dr G. E. Goodfellow:

Am a practicing physician and surgeon in Tombstone where I reside. Saw Morgan S. Earp on last Saturday, March 18, 1882, after he was shot, saw him on the floor of Campbell & Hatch's saloon in this place. He was in a state of collapse resulting from a gunshot, or pistol wound, entering the body just to the left of the spinal column in the region of the left kidney emerging on the right side of the body in the region of the gall bladder. It certainly injured the great vessels of the body causing hemorrhage which, undoubtedly, causes death. It also injured the spinal column. It passed through the left kidney and also through the loin. In my opinion it was necessarily a fatal wound. I know nothing of the circumstances connected with the reception of the wound. He lived from half to three-fourths of an hour after I saw him.

11. Mrs. Marietta D. Spence, wife of Pete Spence, gave very important testimony at the coroner's Inquest held on Morgan Earp's body. Beyond any reasonable question it demonstrated who the killers were:

Marietta D. Spence, being sworn testifies as follows: Reside in Tombstone and am wife of Peter Spence; on last Saturday, the 18th of March, was in my home on Fremont street; for two days my husband was not home, but in Charleston, but came home about 12 o'clock p.m. Saturday. He came with two parties, one named Freis, a German; I don't know the other's name but he lives in the house of Manuel Acusto. Each one had a rifle. Immediately arriving he sent a man to take care of the horses and take them to the house of Manuel Acusto. Then they entered the front room and began to converse with Frank Stilwell. When they had finished, Frank Stilwell went out and Spence went to bed. This all happened that night. Spence remained in bed until 9 o'clock a.m. Sunday. Freis slept there. The other man went to his house on Friday and stayed all day; went out Friday night but returned in a short time to sleep.

Saturday he was out all day and up to 12 o'clock at night, when Spence came in. There was an Indian with Stilwell called Charley. He was armed with a pistol and a carbine. He left Saturday morning with Stilwell and came back with him at 12 o'clock at night. Both Charley and Stilwell were armed with pistols and carbines when they returned to the house Saturday night. The conversation between Spence and Stilwell and the others was carried on in a low tone. They appeared to be talking some secret. When they came in I got out of bed to receive them and noticed they were excited, why I don't know.

Stilwell came into the house about an hour before Spence and the other two. Stilwell brought me a dispatch from Spence, saying he would be up from Charleston that night, Saturday; [received it about two p.m.]. Think Spence left last night, the 20th, for Sonora. Don't know positively that he went. On Sunday morning Spence told me to get breakfast about six o'clock——which I did, after we had a quarrel during which he struck me and my mother and during which he threatened to shoot me, when my mother told him he would have to shoot her too. His expression was that if I said a word about something I knew that he would kill me; that he was going to Sonora and would leave my dead body behind him.

Spence didn't tell me so but I know he killed Morgan Earp; I think he did it because he arrived at the house all of a tremble, and both the others who came with him. Spence's teeth were chattering when he came in. I asked him if he wanted something to eat and he said he did not. Myself and mother heard the shots and it was a little after when Stilwell and the Indian, Charley, came in, and from one-half to three-quarters of an hour after Spence and the other two men came. I think that Spence and the other two men, although they might have arrived during the night, had left their horses outside of town, and after the shooting had gone and got them. I judged they had been doing wrong from the condition, white and trembling, in which they arrived. Spence and the two men had been for several days in the habit of leaving home in the middle of the day and returning in the middle of the night, but they never returned in the same condition as they did on that night, and after hearing the next morning of Earp's death, I came to the conclusion that Spence and the others had done the deed. Have not seen the Indian, Charley, since that night; do not know where he is.

James C. Earp is buried in the Mountain View Cemetery of San Bernardino, California, Lot no. 5, Block "Bubah."

Four days ago while Mother and myself were standing at Spence's house, talking with Spence and the Indian, Morgan Earp passed by, when Spence nudged the Indian and said, "That's him, that's him." The Indian then started down the street so as to get ahead of him and get a good look at him. Freis is a German who works for Acusto as teamster. Think he was with Spence Saturday night and assisted in killing Earp, also Stilwell and Indian Charley.

The Coroner's Jury evidently agreed with Mrs. Spence's idea as to the identity of the slayers of Morgan Earp. After listening to the testimony of ten sworn witnesses, the jury's verdict was as follows:

I hereby certify that the following annexed papers, contain a transcript of the testimony submitted to a jury of inquest impanelled by me as coroner of Chocise County, A.T., in the town of Tombstone A.T. on March 19, 1882, to inquire into where, when, and by what means, one Morgan S. Earp came to his death. And that the findings of the same jury was that his death was caused, as they believe, from the effect of a gunshot, or pistol wound, on the night of March 18, 1882, by Peter Spence, Frank Stilwell, and John Doe Freis and an Indian called Charlie and another Indian name unknown.

12. Deputy United States Marshal Wyatt Earp rode into the Dragoon Mountains with a posse and killed the half-breed Florentino, one of those accused of killing Morgan Earp.

13. James Earp described the conditions in Tombstone, March 1882, very well. Of particular interest is his estimation of the population of the town as being "between four and five thousand." This figure being far short of the ten to fifteen thousand that fiction writers usually record. The Federal 1880 Census lists the inhabitants of Tombstone as numbering 5,300.

Chapter 5

VIRGIL TALKS

Virgil Earp was interviewed by a reporter in San Francisco. The Arizona DAILY STAR carried the story in its May 30, 1882, issue.

The San Francisco *Examiner* of the 27th contains an interview with Virgil Earp, from which the following extracts are made: "I was born in Kentucky but was raised in Illinois and Iowa.[1] My parents came to this state, settling in San Bernardino, near Colton, at which later place they now live. I served for a little over three years in the war, in an Illinois regiment,[2] and then came to California in 1866.[3] I soon went into New Mexico, Arizona and all that southern country, where I have spent nearly six years. When Tombstone was discovered I was in Prescott. The first stage that went out of Prescott toward Tombstone was robbed. Robberies were frequent and became expensive, and the disordered condition of the new country soon brought a demand for the better protection of business and money, as well as life. I was asked to go to Tombstone in my capacity as United States Marshal, and went.[4] My brother Wyatt and myself were fairly well treated for a time, but when the desperate characters who were congregated there, and who had been unaccustomed to troublesome molestation by the authorities, learnt that we meant business and determined to stop their rascality, if possible, they began to make it warm for us. The Tombstone country is of a peculiar character, the community being unsettled and dangerous. Most of the business men there stayed simply to make money enough to live somewhere else comfortably, and of course the greatest object with them is to have as much money as possible spent in the town and to get as much of it as they can,[5] careless of the means of dispensation or the results of rough manners. Aside from the legitimate business men the bulk of the residents are idle or desperate characters, most of them coming into town broke and depending upon the gambling tables or criminal ventures to supply them with means of livelihood and dissipation.

THE COWBOYS

numbered at one time nearly 200 but during the last two years about fifty of them have been killed. The most of them are what we call "saddlers," living almost wholly in the saddle and largely engaged in raiding into Sonora and adjacent country and stealing cattle, which they sell in Tombstone. It is rarely that any of these stolen cattle are recovered. When the thieves are closely pursued and it seems likely that they will be overhauled and the stock recovered, the cowboys sell the cattle to some of the butchers practically in partnership with them, and I know of cases where the finest cattle in the country have been sold at a dollar a head. When cattle are not handy the cowboys rob stages and engage in similar enterprises to raise money. As soon as they are in funds they ride into town, drink, gamble and fight. They spend their money as free as water in the saloons, dancehouses or faro banks, and this is one reason they have so many friends in town. All that large class of degraded characters who gather the crumbs of such carouses stand ready to assist them out of any trouble or into any paying rascality. The saloons and gambling houses, into whose treasuries most of the money is ultimately turned, receive them cordially and must be called warm friends of the cowboys. A good many of the merchants fear to express themselves against the criminal element because they want to keep the patronage of the cowboys' friends, and the result is that when any conflict between the officers and cattle thieves or stage robbers occurs, followed up by shootings around town, as witnessed during the last few months, most of the expression of opinion comes from the desperado class and their friends, and the men who should speak loudest and most decisively to correct the condition of affairs are generally the quietest. An officer doing his duty must rely almost entirely upon his own conscience for encouragement. The sympathy of the respectable portion of the community may be with him but it is not openly expressed.

THE BAD ELEMENT

knows its advantage in this respect, and makes the most of it. The cowboys are collected from all parts of the Western country, from which they have been crowded by advancing civilization, and they know that Arizona is about the only place left for them to operated in as an organization. With a complete breaking up of their company threatened in event of losing their hold where they are now, they resist official interference with the greatest desperation.[6] Concerning the fights between the cowboys and myself and brothers, it has been stated over and over again that there was an old feud between us and some of our enemies, and that we were fighting only to revenge personal wrongs and gratify personal hatred. All such statements are false.[7] We went into Tombstone to do our duty as officers. To do that we were put in conflict with a band of desperadoes, and it resolved itself into a question of which side could first drive the other out of the country, or kill them in it. Today my brother Morg is dead and I am a cripple for life. My other brothers are fugitives, but they will give themselves up. It was our boys who killed Stillwell *[sic]*.

BEFORE STILLWELL *[sic]* DIED

he confessed that he killed Morg and gave the names of those who were implicated with him. When my brothers were leaving Arizona they got dispatches from Tucson saying that Stillwell and a party of friends were watching all the railroad trains passing that way, and they were going through them in search of all Earps and their friends, carrying shotguns under their overcoats and promising to kill on sight. Our boys were bound to look out for themselves, and when they got near Tucson were very cautious. They found Stillwell near the track and killed him.[8] For the first time the Sheriff has shown anxiety to arrest someone, and the boys are keeping out of his way. The Court in Tombstone does not sit again for six months yet, and they don't want to lie in jail all that time waiting for trial, but when the Court sits again they will give themselves up, and, with fair play, will be acquitted. The press dispatches that have been sent here have been very unfair to us and have been made to conform to a plan to carry all these fights into politics this season.[9] I am a Republican. My brothers are Democrats. I am sorry to see the thing taken into politics as a personal measure, because the true aspect of the trouble will be lost and new enmities are likely to be created. I heard that Doc Holliday, one of our friends about whom there has been considerable talk, had been captured at Denver. Word was sent to me that he would be taken out on a writ of *habeas corpus*, and that before an officer from the Territory could reach him he would be released. I do not know if he succeeded in getting off or not. There was

SOMETHING VERY PECULIAR

about Doc. He was gentlemanly, a good dentist, a friendly man, and yet outside of us boys I don't think he had a friend in the Territory. Tales were told that he had murdered men in different parts of the country; that he had robbed and committed all manner of crimes, and yet when persons were asked how they knew it they could only admit that it was hearsay, and that nothing of the kind could really be traced up to Doc's account.[10] He was a slender, sickly fellow, but whenever a stage was robbed or row started, and help was needed, Doc was one of the first to saddle his horse and report for duty. The stories, at one time widely circulated, that we were in with the cowboys and quarreled over division of the spoils, was ridiculous. It was at least disbelieved by Wells, Fargo & Co., who I represented, and while I was City Marshal they gave me this." The speaker here displayed on the inside of his coat a large gold badge, a five pointed star set inside of a circular band, inscribed on one side, "City Marshal, Tombstone, A.T.," and on the other, "V. W. Earp, with Compliments of Wells, Fargo & Co."[11] Mr. Earp was in such pain that for the time his story was cut short. He was met by two friends, who accompanied him to this city, where he will remain about thirty days. Yesterday he was placed under the care of a leading surgeon, and was unable to receive visitors, keeping himself well secluded. His escape from death by his last wounds was remarkable. Besides the shot which crippled his arm, he was shot clean through the body, and upon the day following that upon which the dead body of his brother reached the home of his parents, he,

*Virgil Walter Earp,
Tombstone's Chief
of Police and
Deputy United
States Marshal.*

too, arrived at Colton, expecting to die. Though in good health
otherwise, his arm will prevent any further active participation in
the sensational warfare against the cowboys.[12]

HISTORICAL NOTES AND EDITORIAL COMMENTS

1.   Virgil Walter Earp was born July 18, 1843, in Ohio County,
Kentucky. He was the second of eight children to be born to Nicholas P.,
and Virginia Ann Earp. Most of Virgil's boyhood was spent in the Pella, Iowa, area where he grew accustomed to both farm and city life.

Two of the more important events that molded the young Virgil's
life were his marriage to Ellen Rysdam, a Dutch girl, and his subsequent en-
listment in the Union Army. Both events were related although they happened almost a year apart. The later action was devised as a way of escaping the
undesirable aspects of the former, ill-considered act.

A letter in the editor's possession, Bertrand to Irvine, October 21, 1958, recounts the story of these two important events in Virgil's life:

Mazama Lodge
October 21, 1958

Mrs. Irvine
17007 S.E. Oatfield Road
Milwaukie, Oregon

Dear Mrs. Irvine:

. . . . You state that you have the records of the Bertrands' and Aubichon's. What do they have to do with the Earp Clan?

The only connection that they have is thru the marriage of my grandfather to the granddaughter of Virgil Earp. Where does the interest of this lineage enter the records?

Now to get back to the Earps. Shortly after the war II, I was talking to my foster mother, who was Nellie Jane Law Bohn's half-sister, about her mother and the marriage to Virgil Earp. This is what she told me.

Ellen Rysdam and Virgil Earp had been keeping company for quite some time when they decided to marry. Ellen's folks when approached about it, flew into a rage and forbid her to marry below her station in life. They also insisted that they stop their courtship and to never see each other again. Of course this merely threw them together closer and the first time that they could slip away, they did so. Their marriage was made in secret in one of the adjoining counties and then kept secret until such time as when she became pregnant. [They did not "slip away to an adjoining county to be married." The ceremony was performed in Knoxville, which was the county seat of Marion County, about 25 miles from Pella, their home town. The marriage was effectively concealed when the young couple changed their names. Virgil called himself Walter Earp, and Ellen used the name Ellen Donahoo.] At the same time, the Civil War broke out and to escape the wrath of her father, Virgil joined the service with his brothers or brother. [Virgil returned to Monmouth, Illinois and joined up.] Father Rysdam tried to have the marriage annulled but because he couldn't find out where they had been married failed [sic]. This being due to the fact that Ellen refused to tell him where they were married. When Virgil's efforts to contact Ellen by mail came into being, again Father Rysdam interfered. Then someone returned from the front and told the story that Virgil had died in one of the training camps and that he had seen him buried. Of course this brought about the opportunity for Father Rysdam to step in and insist on the marriage of his choice. The Van Rossen marriage. Ellen and her child soon became Van Rossens whereupon they then started out west.

Later on as they were passing thru Idaho, the wagon train had an opportunity to do some trading with Chief Joseph and his braves. Not having seen a towheaded youngster before, Chief Joseph caught a glimpse of Nellie Jane and immediately set out to try and trade for her. He wanted to have her as his daughter and would trade more ponies and skins than was ever offered by him on any occasion of trading. Of course it was refused and he was told the reason so as to

The home of Virgil Earp as it appears in Tombstone today. (Turner Collection).

not offend him. During their stay at this site of trading Chief Joseph came many times to play with and hold the little girl that was to become my Great Grandmother.

This story was also one of the tales that my Great Grandmother told me as a child.

Ironically, had she been taken by Joseph, she would have had the opportunity to have seen her own father, without knowing it, at a time when he came to the great chief's camp to pick up a white renegade that was being held for the Wyatt Earp *[sic]*.

As it was, it wasn't until she had been married and had her own family that she saw for the first time, Virgil Earp her real father.

That meeting was a tale told by "Murmur" Jane, Nellie Jane Law Bohn.

As the years passed, Nellie Jane married and had her family and then acquired a new son-in-law. She had heard the stories of these famous lawmen named Earp and began to wonder as to the relationship to the Earps that was her father. As she wondered about this she discussed it with her new son-in-law Alex Bertrand and they decided to write and find out about it. He took some time and found out from some friends as to where to write. This done they waited for their letter to be answered. Soon a letter from Virgil arrived and it was filled to the brim with questions as to where she was born and what was the name of her mother, was her mother alive and where did she live, etc. Murmer Jane answered immediately with all the information that could be crammed into the limits of a letter. A few days after she posted the letter by fastest post, she received a telegram from Virgil Earp that he was her father and would be up to see her as soon as he could manage, which was very soon.

She was very excited over these new developments and had overlooked the legal potential that this brought about for her mother, and half-brothers and sisters. Well, amidst this harangue that she received from these people, she made her way to the railroad station and met her father for the first time in their lives. It was a meeting of great feelings and after these had been dispensed with, they went to her home. There she sat up late at night with her father and he would recould the happenings of his life after his entrance to serve in the Civil War.

During his visit, he met his former wife Ellen and it was decided that due to the fact that both thought the other dead and had married again that it was best to let it remain so to continue their lives as it was. As for the legal entity, there was a law being passed where it entitled one to assume that the other was legally dead by the rights of which is now regarded as the Statute of Limitations. Therefore, each remained in their respective positions without legal entanglement and as friends to the grave. It is to be remembered that theirs wasn't the only marriage that was so entangled. For during the Civil War, many homes and families were involved in just such a manner due to the inaccuracy of the war records of those days. In fact some of our many prominent families of this day bear the stigma such as this was. . . . .

Respectfully yours,
George Bertrand
Mazama Lodge
Government Camp, Oregon

2. Virgil Earp served as a private in Company C, 83rd Regiment, Illinois Infantry. He enlisted July 26, 1862, and was discharged June 24, 1865, at the age of 22. In spite of the fact that Nicholas P. Earp, his father, was the Provost Marshal in Pella, Virgil went to Monmouth, Illinois, and enlisted. This is good evidence that Virgil was fleeing from the wrath of Father Rysdam, who was mad at the young man for transforming his daughter into a wife and expectant mother.

3. Nicholas P. Earp had been the captain of a wagon train that left Pella, Iowa, in 1864 bound for the San Bernardino area of southern California. For details of the trip see the *Rousseau Diary: Across the Desert to California, In 1864.* The diary is in two sections: Pella, Iowa, to Salt Lake, and Salt Lake to San Bernardino. The second section can be obtained in printed form from the San Bernardino County Museum Association. Mr. Earp described the southern California area as "a lush farming paradise" in a letter, Nicholas P. Earp to James Copla, April 2, 1865, (available at the Colton Public Library, Colton, California).

About a year after Virgil was discharged from the service, in June of 1865, he arrived at his father's home in California.

Alvira Earp, wife of Virgil Earp. (Glenn G. Boyer Collection).

4. Virgil Walter Earp was appointed Deputy United States Marshal on November 27, 1879, by Crawley P. Dake, Arizona's Territorial Marshal, whose headquarters were at Prescott, which was the capital. When the Earp party reached Tucson the local deputy marshal scratched out the word "Yavapai" on Virgil's commission and added the word "Pima." Virgil was now an official Deputy U. S. Marshal in Pima County. It is interesting to note that Virgil, not Wyatt, took the commission to Tombstone. (See, Chapter 1, Note 11.)

5. This description of Tombstone's economy is very good, and actually would fit the conditions found in almost every mining boom town in the West.

6. Virgil Earp's description of the serious international problems brought about by organized bands of criminals operating from both sides of the line, is perhaps, the most accurate to be recounted about conditions that existed at that date. A group of approximately 200 loosely organized "saddlers" (generally know as "cowboys") provided Arizona's contribution to the area of criminal activities; while various gangs of Mexican banditti engaged in all kinds of illegal skulduggery and murder. So serious was the situation that officials feared a break in relations between the United States and Mexico.

The Earps were obviously facing serious problems in southeastern Arizona. Their recourse to six-shooter law, however, was an effective tool in breaking up "cowboy" rule. The killing of Billy Clanton, Tom and Frank McLaury, Curly Bill Brocius, Frank Stilwell, and John Ringo, proclaimed in a meaningful manner: "Rustler leave, or be killed." Lesser gang members, fearing the wrath of the Earps, fled into Mexico or northern Arizona.

Governor John C. Fremont called attention to this lawless condition in southeastern Arizona in a speech to the assembly of the eleventh Territorial Legislature. See, George H. Kelley, *Legislative History Arizona*, 1864-1912, pp. 98-99.

> February 21, 1881:
> I have to ask the earnest attention of the council to the conditions of southeastern Arizona and the Mexican border, which requires immediate action from the executive authority of the territory. It is well known to the Legislative Assembly that life and property on both sides of the line are insecure, and to prevent the rapid increase of this insecurity and danger, decided measures must be adopted to break up and destroy the organized bands of outlaws which now infest the region, to the great danger and detriment of our citizens and to the manifest risk of serious complications with the government of the United States.

The General Services Administration, National Archives and Records Service, Washington, D. C. 10408 contains some valuable correspondence (National Archives Record Group 60, 68 pages) that relates to the "cowboy" troubles on the Mexican border, the work of the Earp brothers in suppressing lawlessness, and the Department of Justice investigation of Arizona's marshal, C. P. Dake. From among these valuable documents the following two letters have been chosen to corroborate Virgil Earp's opinion of the cowboys and the border trouble:

S. F. Phillips (Acting Attorney General) to the Honorable James G. Blaine (United States Secretary of State), November 17, 1881, letter:

> I have the honor to acknowledge the receipt of your letter of the 15th inst. with enclosures; relative to the lawlessness that exists on the southern border of Arizona Territory, and to inform you that in compliance with your request, I have instructed the Marshal of Arizona (Marshal C. P. Dake) and his deputies to cooperate to the fullest extent and in every proper way with the officers of the Territory, in earnest endeavors to suppress the disorders that prevail therein to arrest the guilty parties, and bring them speedily to justice.

Joseph Boyer, the manager of Texas Consolidated Mining and Smelting Company, Galeyville, to the Honorable John J. Gosper who was the acting Governor of the Arizona Territory, September 17, 1881. The letter is printed as written.

> In reply to your inquiry yesterday concerning the "cow Boys" who are reported to have been and still are raiding along the line of Sonora and Arizona——I will say——The gang who are known as "cow

*Nicholas Porter Earp and Virginia Earp, parents of the Earp
brothers. (Arizona Historical Society).*

*John H. (Doc)
Holliday, friend
and ally of the
Earps.*

Boys" are engaged in stock raising in the valleys of San Simon and
Cloverdale in the southeastern portion of Arizona, and from good
authority I learn that the cattle, horses and sheep now controlled by
said "cow boys" have been stolen from the citizens of Sonora and
Arizona and New Mexico: they are reported to have about 300 head
of cattle at or near Granite Gap in New Mexico and close to the line
of Arizona.

It is a well known fact that they are in the habit of making
raids along the border. Until recently it has been the custom to steal
cattle and horses in Arizona, and drive them into Sonora for sale, and
on the return trip steal stock in Sonora and drive them into Arizona
and New Mexico for sale. Consequently quite a traffic was kept up:
This practice has abated somewhat lately on account of the killing
of 4 "cow boys" at Fronteras in I think June last; the circumstances
as near as can be ascertained is this:

Last spring George Turner and M. McCalister, two well known
cow boys obtained the contract at Fort Bowie for furnishing beef to
the command——they and two assistants went to Sonora to either buy
or steal beef cattle, they succeeded in driving a large herd as far as
Fronteras, where they were attacked by the Mexican citizens, they the
"cow boys" were all killed and one Mexican citizen was killed. Upon

the bodies of Turner and McCalister were found the money which they evidently took to purchase cattle, which amount compared with what they were known to have started from here with proved that the cattle they were driving had not been paid for——this affair has caused bad blood between the "cow boys" and the citizens of Sonora.*Each party taking revenge upon the other whenever opportunity occurs—— consequently it is unsafe for any person to travel the border.

About a month ago the "cow boys" went across the border into Sonora and seeing a good sized pack train in charge of Mexicans, laid in ambush, and at the word of command made a dash and succeeded in capturing the whole outfit, consisting of about $4,000—in Mexican coin, silver bullion, mescal, horses, and cattle: one of the boys in relating to me the circumstances said it was the d____st lot of truck he ever saw——he showed me a piece of bullion I should judge it to be one-half gold. Upon my telling him that trouble would likely arise from this, he replied that it was a smuggling train and they would not dare say much——there was 3 Mexicans killed in the affray.

A notorious "cow boy" known as John R. [John Ringo] offers to sell all the mutton the town can consume at the rate of $1.00 per head——no secrecy is observed in these kinds of transactions——as regard the local officers of the law. I cannot do better than refer you to the clipping from the *Arizona Star* of September 10, 1881, which is hereunto attached.

A Galeyville "Dogberry"

How Justice is Sometimes Dispensed on the Border.

EDITOR STAR: Permit me to give you a brief history of a trial before a border Justice of the Peace, known as G. W. Ellingwood.

David Estis was one of two men who robbed a game of about four hundred dollars in cash at the midnight hour in the town of Galeyville, as follows: Estis entered the front door of the saloon in which the game was being played, armed with a Winchester and six-shooter, his "pal" passing in at the rear of the house, armed in a similar manner. They ordered the players to throw up their hands and surrender all their cash. This accomplished, Estis proceeded to the corral of Babcock & Co. and extracted and confiscated a valuable horse, making the total clean up about $500. Estis was subsequently arrested by Deputy Sheriff Goodman and tried before said Ellingwood and discharged. His Honor ruled in the examination of the witness that they could not testify to the taking of money (ordered by the bandits to be left on the table) unless they of their own knowledge knew to whom a particular parcel of money belonged. This could not be proven, absquatulate instantly. Thus you see a single pair in Galeyville wins $500.

Under the ruling of this astute and noble Judge no evidence was admitted necessary to conviction. Sheriff Goodman asked to be sworn to testify that the prisoner offered him $500 to cast loose his shackels and let him at liberty. This testimony was ruled out by the court as being irrelevant and not material to the issue.

While the trial was in progress the Judge stated to Quartz Johnson that the prisoner could not be convicted, and subsequently that he (the Judge) would now stand well with the cowboys. Respectfully,
                                                                CLIPPER.

Galeyville, Sept. 4.

I will also state another case——"Billy the Kid" a stripling belonging to the profession was arrested for stealing horses. Upon his examination the court ruled that the affidavit upon which he was arrested charged him with the crime of theft, while the statutes showed no such a crime——but should have been larceny——also the person from whom the horses had been stolen voluntarily stated to the court that he did not want the boy prosecuted as he agreed to return the horses ——the same person told me afterward that if he prosecuted the boy, the other cow boys would steal every head of stock he had. Which he being a poor man could not afford to stand.

The cow boys frequently visit our town and often salute us with an indiscriminate discharge of firearms——and after indulging in a few drinks at the saloons, practice shooting at the lamps, bottles, glasses, etc.——sometimes going to the length of shooting the cigar out of ones mouth. This of course produces a nervous feeling among visitors especially.

The situation at the writing is not materially changed from the above.

The "cow boys" as a class are not overly brave, though there are some among them who have gone through so much difficulty that they have become desperate and will take desperate chances.

As regards my standing and position, I will state that at present I am the acting manager of the Texas Consolidated Mining and Smelting Company: and would refer you to Hon. William Springer of Illinois as to the general facts stated above,who probably remembers the situation as it appeared to him at the time of his visit here during the early part of this season.

As to my character for truth and veracity I take pleasure in referring you to Hon. George Anislie delegate to Congress from Idaho.

And now in conclusion I will state that at any time you feel that I can give information which would assist you, I will upon receipt of ——forward you all the facts I may be in possession of.

I have the honor to be your very humble servant.

JOSEPH BOYER.

7. The feud between the Earps and the Clantons did not begin until the brother of the McLaury boys, a Fort Worth attorney, came to Tombstone to avenge his brothers' deaths. (See, Chapter 1, Note 2.)

8. The killing of Frank Stilwell by Deputy United States Marshal Earp's posse has not been completely detailed because the Coroner's Inquest has disappeared from the Pima County Courthouse. Fortunately, however, the Arizona *Weekly Citizen* printed the inquest in full. See, "The Stilwell Inquest," *Weekly Citizen*, Sunday, April 2, 1882, (on file with the Arizona Historical Society). See, Chapter 1, Note 20.

If Frank Stilwell confessed to the Earp party, he did it in a hurry, because they did not give him much time before shooting him.

9. The press dispatches that were wired to San Francisco, where Virgil Earp was seeking medical aid, were very unfair because they had their origins in either the Tombstone *Nugget* or the Tucson *Star*, both newspapers were anti-Earp and supported the cattlemen, the rustlers, and the County Ring.

Virgil Earp is buried at the Riverview Cemetery in Portland, Oregon. (Turner Collection).

10. Doc Holliday had a reputation of being a killer, but this record is rather difficult to substantiate with factual evidence. He probably did all of his killing in Tombstone, although he may have exchanged shots ineffectively with a man or two in Texas. Doc killed Tom and Frank McLaury in the so-called "O.K. Corral," fight and later helped Wyatt Earp's Deputy U. S. Marshal's posse kill Frank Stilwell, Florentino, and Curly Bill Brocius.

In 1884, he seriously wounded Billy Allen in a gunfight in Leadville, Colorado. Newspaper reports of this shooting may be read in the *Leadville Democrat*, "Holliday Shoots," August 23, 1884, and the Tucson *Daily Citizen*, "Doc Holliday," April 2, 1885.

Without question Holliday was willing to fight with almost no provocation but there is substantial evidence he was a poor shot, at least while drunk. See, Chapter 1, Note 8.

11. Virgil Earp as deputy United States marshal in the Tombstone area during the period of November 27, 1879 through December 29, 1881, rendered valuable service to Wells, Fargo and Company. This badge was a token of their trust and appreciation. See, the Tombstone *Epitaph*, July 6, 1972.

The badge has been passed down through Virgil Earp's family to Mrs. Hildreth Halliwell, who was Allie Earp's grand-niece.

12. In spite of his handicap Virgil was elected marshal of the city of Colton, California, and served as a deputy sheriff in Goldfield, Nevada.

Chapter 6
WYATT TELLS OF RIDING SHOTGUN

The Sunday Edition of the San Francisco EXAMINER for August 9, 1896, featured an interview with Wyatt Earp where he described some of his experiences riding shotgun for Wells Fargo in Arizona fifteen years earlier.

With his gun across his knee, his treasure box under his feet and his eyes peering into every patch of chaparral by the roadside, the shotgun messenger played an humble but important part in the economy of frontier life.

Humble did I say? Well, yes, for there was far more of danger than of profit or honor attached to the work. And yet such a man as a big express company would be sure to single out for the safeguarding of the treasure entrusted to it must need be a man fitted to fight his way to the top in a community where the sheer scorn of death was the only safeguard of life. So at least it would seem. But of the many daring spirits that I have known to imperil their lives in the Wells-Fargo messenger service I can recall only one who clambered to any eminence out of the hurly-burly of frontier life. And even then it was no very dizzy height that he reached. Bob Paul, as fearless a man and as fast a friend as I ever knew, graduated from a messengership to the shrievalty of Pima County, Arizona, and from that to the United States Marshalship of the territory.[1]

Lucky Bob Paul. In fancy I see him, his always well-nourished frame endowed with "fair round belly with fat capon lined," overseeing his smelting works in Tucson, and telling a younger generation about the killing of Bud Philpott.

Bud Philpott used to drive the stage from Tombstone to Tucson, when that was the terminus of the Southern Pacific. Later when the railroad reached as far as Benson, Bud's daily drive was only twenty-eight instead of 110 miles——for which, you may be sure, Bud was duly thankful. The worst part of the road was where it skirted the San Pedro river. There the track was all sandy and cut up, which made traveling about as exhilarating as riding a rail. But that didn't perturb Bud half as much as the prospect of a hold-up. That prospect increased by an alarming arithmetical ratio when the boom struck Tombstone and the worst cutthroats on the frontier poured into the camp by hunddreds.

Come to think of it, it takes some sand to drive a stage through that kind of country, with thousands of dollars in the front boot and the chance of a Winchester behind every rock. Of course, the messenger had his gun and his six-shooter, and he is paid to fight. The driver is paid to drive and it takes him all his time to handle the lines without thinking of shooting. That was why I always made allowances for Bud as I sat beside him, admiring the accuracy with which he would flick a sandfly off the near leader's flank or plant a mouthful of tobacco juice in the heart of a cactus as we jolted past it, but never relaxing my lookout for an ambuscade. Indeed I often wondered that we were such good friends, considering that I as custodian of the treasure box, would infallibly draw what fire there was around Bud Philpott's massive pink ears.

That is part of the cursedness of the shotgun messenger's life——the loneliness of it. He is like a sheep dog, feared by the flock and hated by the wolves. On the stage he is a necessary evil. Passengers and driver alike regard him with aversion, without him and his pestilential box their lives would be ninety per cent safer and they would know it. The bad men, the rustlers—— the stage robbers actual and potential——hate him. They hate him because he is the guardian of property, because he stands between them and their desires, because they will have to kill him before they can get their hands into the coveted box. Most of all they hate him because of his shotgun——the homely weapon that makes him the peer of many armed men in a quick turmoil of powder and lead.

The Wells-Fargo shotgun is not a scientific weapon. It is not a sportsmanlike weapon. It is not a weapon wherewith to settle an affair of honor between gentlemen. But, oh!, in the hands of an honest man hemmed in by skulking outlaws it is a sweet and a thrice blessed thing. The express company made me a present of the gun with which they armed me when I entered their service, and I have it still. In the severe code of ethics maintained on the frontier such a weapon would be regarded as legitimate only in the service for which it was designed, or in defense of an innocent life encompassed by superior odds. But your true rustler throws such delicate scruples to the wind. To him a Wells-Fargo shotgun is a most precious thing, and if by hook or crook —mostly crook—he can possess himself of one he esteems himself a king among his kind. Toward the end of my story last Sunday I described the killing of Curly Bill. By an inadvertency I said that he opened fire on me with a Winchester. I should have said a Wells-Fargo shotgun. Later I will tell you where Curly Bill got that gun.

The barrels of the important civilizing agent under consideration are not more than two-thirds the length of an ordinary gun barrel.[2] That makes it easy to carry and easy to throw upon the enemy, with less danger of wasting good lead by reason of the muzzle catching in some vexatious obstruction. As the gun has to be used quickly or not at all, this shortness of barrel is no mean advantage. The weapon furthermore differs from the ordinary gun in being much heavier as to barrel, thus enabling it to carry a big charge of buckshot. No less than twenty-one buckshot are loaded into each barrel.[3] That means a shower of forth-two leaden messengers, each fit to take a man's life or break a bone if it should reach the right spot. And as the buckshot scatters literally the odds are all in its favor. At close quarters the charge will convert a man into a most unpleasant mess, whereof Curly Bill was a conspicuous example. As for range—well, at one hundred yards, I have killed a coyote with one of these guns, and what will kill a coyote will kill a stage robber any day.

I have said that I made allowances for poor Bud Philpott. What I mean is that I forgave him for his well-defined policy of peace at any price. Whereof I will narrate an example not wholly without humor at the expense of us both. We were bowling along the road to Benson one morning when four men jumped suddenly out of the brush that skirted the road a short distance ahead of us, and took their station, two on one side of the road and two on the other.

*Wyatt with a Wells Fargo
sawed-off shotgun that
he used to kill Curly Bill.*

JIM
EARLE
NOV 73

"My God, Wyatt, we're in for it!" gasped Bud, ducking forward instinctively and turning an appealing look on me. "What shall we do?"

"There's only one thing to be done," I said. He saw what I meant by the way I handled the gun.

"Ye ain't surely going to make a fight of it, are ye, Wyatt?" he said anxiously. "It looks kinder tough."

"Certainly I am," I said, feeling to see that my six-shooters were where I wanted 'em. "Now listen. The minute they holler 'Halt!' you fall down in the boot, but for God's sake keep hold of the lines. I'll take the two on the left first, and keep the second barrel for the pair on your side."

*The ruins of Drew's Station along the Kinnear and Company
stagecoach route. (Glenn G. Boyer Collection)*

Now all this had passed very quickly and we were bearing down on the strangers at a steady lope. Bud groaned. "I'll do what you say," he protested, "but if I was you I'd let 'em have the stuff, and then catch 'em afterwards."

As we got within range of the four men I threw my gun on them. Even as I did so it flashed across me that they wore no masks; that their faces were wondrously pacific, and that no sign of a gun peeped out among them. Just as I realized that we had been fooled, the four threw up their hands with every appearance of terror, their distended eyes fastened on the muzzle of my gun, their lips moving in voluble appeals for mercy. Bud jammed down the brake and jerked the team onto their haunches, showering valient curses on the men to whom he had proposed to surrender a moment before.

They were harmless Mexicans who had been searching the brush for some strayed broncos. The impulse that led them to plant themselves by the road on the approach of the stage was sheer idiocy, and they were lucky that it did not cost them their

lives. What they really had intended was to ask us if we had seen
any horses back along the road.

This opera bouffe situation was the nearest approach to
a holdup that came within my experience. My brother Morgan,
who succeeded me, was equally fortunate.[4] After he left the service the post was resumed by Bob Paul, whom I had succeeded at
the time when he retired in order to run for sheriff of Pima
County. And it was then that Bud Philpott ran into the adventure which capped with tragedy our comedy encounter with the
Mexicans.

It was in 1881. The stage left Tombstone at 7 o'clock in
the evening with a full load of passengers inside and out, and a
well-filled treasure box in the front boot. They changed teams as
usual at Drew's Station, fifteen miles out. About three hundred
yards further on the road crosses a deep ravine.[5] Just as the
horses started up the opposite side of this ravine, the coach following them by its own momentum, there came a shout of "Halt
there!" from some bushes on the further bank. Before the driver

could have halted even if he had wanted to, they started in with their Winchesters, and poor Bud Philpott lurched forward with a gurgle in his throat. Before Bob Paul could catch hold of him he fell down under the wheels, dragging the lines with him.

"Halt there!" shouted the robbers again.

"I don't halt for nobody," proclaimed Paul, with a swear word or two, as he emptied both barrels of his gun in the direction the shots came from. His judgement was superior to his grammar, for we learned afterwards that he had wounded one of the rustlers.

Now things happened quickly on the frontier, where bullets count for more than words, and the greatest difficulty I have encountered in the task of writing these recollections is that of trying to convey an idea of the rapidity with which one event follows another.

The moment the first shots were fired and Philpott fell, the horses plunged ahead so viciously that nothing could have stopped them. In missing the messenger and killing the driver the robbers had defeated their own plans. As Bob fired he moved over to Philpott's seat to get his foot on the brake, thinking that it could not possibly improve matters to have the coach overturned while it was under fire. Imagine the horses yanking the coach out of the ravine and tearing off down the road at a breakneck gallop, with the lines trailing about their hoofs. And imagine Bob Paul with his foot on the brake hearing shots and the cries of frightened passengers behind him and wondering what was going to happen next.

What did happen was this: the rustlers had made such elaborate plans for the holdup that they never dreamt of the coach getting away from them. Hence they had tied up their horses in a place where they could not be reached with the speed necessary to render pursuit practicable. With all hope of plunder vanished, and with poor Bud Philpott lying dead in the ravine, these ruffians squatted in the middle of the road and took pot shots at the rear of the coach. Several bullets hit the coach and one mortally wounded an outside passenger.

Such were the coyotes who kenneled in Tombstone during the early '80's. They did this thing deliberately. It was murder for murder's sake——for the mere satisfaction of emptying their Winchesters.

To return to the coach. The horses ran away for two miles but luckily they kept the road, and when they pulled up Bob Paul recovered the lines and drove the rest of the way into Benson, with the dying passenger held upright by his companions on the rear outside seat. The man was a corpse before the journey ended.[6]

At Benson Bob mounted a swift horse and rode back to Tombstone to notify me of the murders. I was dealing faro bank in the Oriental at the time, but I did not lose a moment in setting out on the trail, although faro bank meant anything upwards of $1,000 a night, whereas manhunting meant nothing more than work and cold lead. You see, an affair like that affected me in a double capacity, for I was not only the Deputy United States Marshal for the district,[7] but I continued in the service of the express company as a "private man."

So I organized a posse which included my two brothers. Doc Holliday, Bob Paul and the renowned Bat Masterson[8] — I may have something to say about that prince of frontiersmen at another time—and lost no time in reaching the scene of the shooting. There lay Bud Philpott's body, mangled by the wheels of the coach he had driven so long. And there, among the bushes were the masks the robbers had worn.[9] In the middle of the road we found nearly forty cartridge shells, showing how many shots had been fired in cold blood after the receding coach.

It was easy enough to find the place where their horses had been tied, and from there the trail into the mountains was plain enough. But the story of that chase is too long to be told here. I mentioned last Sunday that it consumed seventeen days, and those who read that narrative will remember that this holdup and that manhunt were the prologue to the bitter and bloody feud that is the central, sombre episode of my thirty years on the frontier.

And now for the story of how Curly Bill became the proud proprietor of a Wells-Fargo shotgun. Charley Bartholomew was a messenger who used to run on the coach from Tombstone to Bisbee. Once every month he was the custodian of a very tidy sum of money sent to pay off the miners. Naturally enough such a prize as that did not escape the attention of such audacious artists in crime as Frank Stilwell, Pete Spence, Pony Deal, and Curly Bill. In fact, the four desperadoes I have named, with one other, planned a masterly holdup which they executed with brilliancy and dash. It happened this way.

The coach carrying the miners' wages had got out of Tombstone about twenty miles when the industrious quintette made their appearance on horseback, three on one side of the road and two on the other. They did not come to close quarters, but kept pace with the coach at a distance of 300 or 400 yards on either side of the road, pumping into it with their Winchesters, and aiming to kill the horses and the messenger. Of course Bartholomew's shotgun might as well have been a blowpipe at that range, and if he had a Winchester with him he did not use it to any effect.

These Indian tactics proved eminently successful in breaking down the nerve of the men on the stage, for after they had run for a mile with an occasional lump of lead knocking splinters out of the coach, Bartholomew told the driver to stop—an injunction which he obeyed very gladly, the robbers came up and made them throw up their hands. They took everything there was to be taken, which amounted to $10,000 and sundries.[10] Among the sundries was Charlie Bartholomew's shotgun with which Curly Bill afterwards tried to fill me full of buckshot, with results fatal to himself. Having marched all hands into the brush the rustlers rode off.

It was not many hours before my brother Morgan and I were on the trail. Two of the men had tied gunny sacks round their horses' hoofs and ridden in the direction of Bisbee, which was twelve miles away. The trail was a difficult one at first, but after a few miles of hard riding the gunny sacks had worn out, and at that point the hoof marks became quite plain. They led directly into Bisbee, to the livery stable kept by Frank Stilwell and Pete Spence. Of course we arrested the pair of them, and they were identified readily enough. As the mails had been robbed I was able to lay a federal charge against them. Stilwell and Spence were still under bonds for trial when my brother Morgan was murdered. And Stilwell was the man who fired the shot. It will be recalled that Stilwell was one of a gang that waylaid me at the depot in Tucson when I was shipping Morgan's body to California, and that he was killed in the attempt. As for Pete Spence, it is only a short time ago that he was released from the penitentiary in Yuma after serving a term for killing a Mexican.[11]

Wyatt Earp as he appeared as a lawman in Dodge City, Kansas, in the late 1870s.

Pony Deal escaped from the scene of the stage robbery into New Mexico, where he was afterward killed while stealing cattle by the gallant Major Fountain, at the head of his rangers. The story of Major Fountain's murder is so recent that I need not repeat it.

There is such an appalling amount of killing in the foregoing two paragraphs that I will turn for what stage folk call "comic relief" to a stage robber whom I had the pleasure of knowing slightly in former years. I met him first in Dodge City, Kansas, and always regarded him as a meritorious and not especially interesting citizen, who was afflicted with a game knee and who spoke with a brogue. Afterward he turned up in Deadwood, when I was there. There were a great many stage robberies around Deadwood at that time, and all the reports had for their central figure a lone road agent, tightly masked, who walked with a limp.

The story one shotgun messenger told me was that, when the coach had halted in response to summons from behind a tree, he plucked up courage to ask the identity of the stranger. Whereupon there came the answer, in the richest of brogues:

"It's Lame Bradley, Knight of the Road. Throw out that box."

The messenger still hesitated whereupon Lame Bradley shot a hole in his ear. The box was thrown down a moment later.

Lame Bradley robbed coach after coach around Deadwood, and then, when suspicion was directed toward him, he returned to Dodge, where he spent money very freely. Afterward he moved to the Panhandle in Texas, where he was killed and robbed by a chum. The chum, by the way, was duly captured and hanged.

Heigh-ho! More killing! And who would ever have expected such garrulity from an old frontiersman? I actually astonish myself.

WYATT EARP

HISTORICAL NOTES AND EDITORIAL COMMENTS

1. Wyatt Earp had a similar ambition to be sheriff in Cochise County. He had failed to get the appointment from Governor Fremont when the county had been formed; but he was campaigning for the office at the upcoming election. This was the reason behind his preposed "deal" with Ike Clanton (the "deal" included Ike Clanton, Billy Clanton, Tom and Frank McLaury, and Joe Hill) and his gang to "turn over" Leonard, Head, and Crane, the Benson stage robbers, so he could arrest them. Wyatt felt that the glory of making the arrest would help him in his bid for sheriff and that the $3,600 reward money offered by Wells Fargo would tempt Ike and his boys. The "deal" seemed to be working and Joe Hill rode into New Mexico to lure the highwaymen into the trap. The "deal," however, failed when Leonard and Head were killed, and Ike Clanton learned that Marshall Williams and Doc Holliday knew about the plot. For a complete explanation of this unsuccessful "deal" see, *Document 94*, Territory of Arizona vs. Morgan Earp, et al. Deposition of Ike Clanton, Deposition of Wyatt Earp, Deposition of Virgil Earp.

2. Wells Fargo used shotguns with both long and short barrels, bored in either 12 or 10 gauge. It was general practice for the express company to use 12 gauge guns for guard duty in the towns, and 10 gauge on the coaches.

3. Shotgun shells at this time were hand loaded in solid brass or copper cartridge cases, usually by the person who fired them. Because of this fact, the grams of powder and the number and size of shot varied in many cases.

4. It is interesting to note that there were no holdups on the stages on which either Wyatt or Morgan Earp were riding shotgun. This, in all probability, meant that the highwaymen preferred not to confront the Earp boys, who had the reputation for being good shots and fearless.

5. Contemporary newspaper accounts located the scene of the March 15, 1881, stage robbery as being at a large wash about 200-300 yards before the coach reached Drew's Station. The ruins of the old stage stop are still standing on the Contention to Benson stage road, about two miles north of Contention City.

6. The dead man was Peter Roerig. He was riding on the top of the coach in the rear outside seat. Newspaper reports made much of the killing of Eli "Bud" Philpott, but little mention was made about Peter Roerig who was also killed by the robbers.

It is interesting to note that Coroner Matthews removed from the body of Peter Reorig seven letters, a book, a pencil, and a check for two dollars; and from the body of Philpott, a silver watch and a number of letters. See, *Document 23, Coroner's Report to Board of Supervisors*, Cochise County Collection: Arizona Historical Society.

7. See Chapter 1, Note 11. Wyatt wasn't made a full time deputy United State Marshal until his brother, Virgil, was seriously wounded on the night of December 28, 1881.

Numerous old-timers have reported that Wyatt Earp was a deputy United States Marshal throughout his Tombstone residence (twenty-eight months). This was not true. These old-timers were either poorly informed or time had dulled their memories. For a typical example, see William Breakenridge's *Helldorado*, p. 111:

> There were a number of killings in Charleston during 1880, but I haven't the names of those killed. A tinhorn gambler, known as "Johnny-behind-the-Deuce," killed Henry Schneid the chief engineer at the smelter, in Quinn's saloon. A mob of the smelter men gathered to lynch him, but the constable [McKelvey] got him into a buckboard behind a span of mules, and started with him for Tombstone as fast as he could go before the mob could organize. The smelter men, to the number of twenty-five or thirty, followed and were overhauling him when he met a man exercising a race mare, and got him to take the prisoner on behind and make a run for Tombstone, as the mules had given out. Here the prisoner was turned over to Wyatt Earp, who was a deputy United States Marshal. When the mob, increased by about an equal number of miners from the Hill, came up to take "Johnny-behind-the-Deuce" away to hang him, Earp stood them off with a shotgun, and dared them to come and get him. . . . .

8. Actually U. S. Marshal Virgil W. Earp and Sheriff John H. Behan both organized posses. Wyatt was a member of his brother's posse, and went as an express company detective, or private officer.

9. Masks such as those described by Wyatt at the robbery scene were to return and haunt him. Big Nosed Kate stated in her memoirs, probably written in 1934 or 1935 while she was a guest of the Pioneer's Home in Prescott, that she had seen a rope mask in Wyatt's trunk while she was visiting Mrs. Earp (Mattie Blaylock). See, A. W. Bork and Glenn G. Boyer, editors, "The O.K. Corral Fight: A Footnote by Kate Elder." *Arizona and the West*, Spring, 1977, p. 77.

> . . . . . also called on Mrs. Wyatt Earp while I was there. Wyatt opened their trunk. Whether it was accidentally, or not, he pulled out a false mustache and a beard. He held it between finger and thumb and turned around toward me and said, "Mrs. Holliday, do you know what these are?" I said, "Yes, I think I do."

The revelation from the trunk was Kate's belated attempt to get back at Wyatt who in all probability had at one time been her boyfriend.

This incident was eagerly seized upon and emphasized by Frank Waters in his book, *The Earp Brothers of Tombstone*, which portrays the Earp brothers in a poor light, as on page 109:

> Then it happened. Kate had been leanin' against the closet door, her hand on the doorknob. As she flipped around the door flew open. There was a bang and a clatter. Out of the closet tumbled a big suitcase spewin' out on the floor some things that made my eyes pop out. Wigs and beards made of unraveled rope and sewn on black cloth masks, some false mustaches, a church deacon's frock coat, a checkered suit like drummers wear, a little bamboo cane——lots of things like that.

It is hard to believe that Frank Waters and Kate Holliday (Kate was known by a variety of names at various times, Elder, Melvin, Fisher, Cummings, and Howard) were describing the same incident. Both people, however, had axes to grind with Earp and Holliday; Waters was developing a fictitious background in order to portray Earp as a tinhorn confidence man, and Kate, while drunk, had accused Holliday with complicity in the Benson stage robbery. While writing her memoirs, fifty-four years later, she had changed her mind saying neither man was involved in either the robbery or the murder.

10. The Tombstone *Epitaph*, September 10, 1881, lists the "take' from the Bisbee stage robbery as being a much smaller amount:

Stage Robbery

> Thursday night, about 10 o'clock, as the stage was nearing Bisbee, being some four or five miles this side in the broken ground, it was stopped by three, some say four, masked men, who, with pistols leveled at the driver and passengers, demanded Wells, Fargo & Co.'s treasure box. The box was thrown out, when they went through the passengers, getting eight dollars and a gold watch from one and about six

hundred dollars from another. From the treasure box they got a fat haul, there was $2,500 in it.

There was a tendency for old-timers to exaggerate the amounts of money taken by stage robbers.

11. Peter Spencer's (Pete Spence) record at Yuma Prison is as follows:

Name: P. M. Spencer   Number: 885
Crime: Assault   Sentence: 5 years
                             from June 10, 1893.

Nearest relative, Mollie E. Spencer, Los Angeles, California. Pardoned unconditionally by Governor L. C. Hughes. This information is from David H. Cruickshanks of London, England.

The San Pedro River near Charleston, Arizona. (The author's collection.)

Chapter 7

WYATT TELLS OF BAT MASTERSON

Wyatt Earp paid tribute to his friend, W. B., "Bat" Masterson, in an interview with the San Francisco EXAMINER published in its Sunday, August 16, 1896, edition.

WYATT EARP'S TRIBUTE TO BAT MASTERSON, THE HERO OF 'DOBE WALLS

Five men, riding to the summit of a knoll, caught sight of a deserted adobe house in a hollow at their feet. As the sun sank toward the edge of the prairie they found their refuge for the night.

The solitude of the building was more painful than the solitude of the plains; the yellowish walls glimmered like the walls of a vault in the gloom that had settled in the hollow as sediment settles in a glass. But these things did not matter, for there was water close by, and those grim walls were thick to stop bullets as well as arrows.

The five men watered their weary horses at the creek, and then drove picket-pins into the ground within a stone's throw of the house, where there was plenty of grass, and tethered the animals thereto with their lariats. Next they unlimbered their heavy saddles and carried them into the house. The plainsman's saddle is more precious to him than jewels. In this case, bacon, coffee and army biscuits were involved. More important still, there was ammunition, and plenty of it.

It was a quarter of a century ago. The five men were scouts, carrying dispatches from Dodge City to Camp Supply, through a country depopulated and laid waste by the Cheyennes. Their camping place was within forty miles of Camp Supply, in the heart of that No-Man's Land known as the Panhandle of Texas.

When the first rays of the sun came slanting over the prairie one of the men went out to water the horses, while his comrades prepared breakfast. Ping! A rifle shot startled the solitude. The four men rushed to the door. The fifth was lying face downward two hundred yards from the house. The horses were plunging and tugging at the ropes. In another second or two they had broken lariats or torn up picket-pins and galloped madly away. A horse can smell an Indian.

Another moment, and a hail of bullets and arrows spattered against the 'dobe walls. Then five hundred yelling Indians galloped from behind a knoll and charged the building.

The four surviving scouts were ready for them. Everything was orderly and precise. It did not need that many words should be spoken. What few laconic orders that were given came from the youngest man in the party. He was a mere boy——a bright, sturdy boy, whose wide, round eyes expressed the alert pugnacity of a blooded bull-terrier. To look at him one could not doubt that nature had molded him for a fighter.

The plan of defense was very simple. Like all buildings in that wild country, the old 'dobe house was provided with portholes on every side. It was a question of shooting fast and shooting straight through those portholes, and the scouts knew how to shoot both fast and straight. The fire was more than the Cheyennes could stand. With a baffled yell they wheeled and retreated, picking up their killed and wounded as they galloped to cover behind one of the many knolls that encompassed the house like the mighty billows of a frozen ocean.

That one charge was the history of the day. It was repeated again and again, first on one side of the house and then on another. Each charge found the scouts prepared, and each time the Indians carried one or more of their dead off the field.

Toward evening there was a brief breathing spell.

"I'm going to bring him," said the youngest scout, the boy with the bull-terrier eyes, pointing at the body lying on its back near the stampeded picket.

"Better not try, Bat, they'll get ye sure."

"We can't leave him lying there like that."

And taking his rifle in his hand the boy went. He ran

out under fire and he staggered back under fire with the body in his arms.

More charges, followed by a sleepless night, to guard against surprises. And at daybreak the fighting began again. Never before were Indians known to make such a stubborn fight. Never before did such a handful hold such a horde at bay. The face of the plain was befreckled with blood up to a radius of fifty yards of the house, but how many dead Indians had been carried off the beleaguered men had no means of knowing. One of them had his leg half shot away and all were sick from exhaustion, when at midafternoon a company of cavalry came riding over the plain and the Indians fled.

Thus was fought the "Battle of 'dobe Walls," the event which made young Bat Masterson a hero on the frontier.[1]

It was not long afterward that Bat drifted to Sweetwater, where he became a lively citizen of as lively a town as ever subsisted on the patronage of a frontier army post. Bat was no more a laggard in love than he was a dastard in war, and Annie Chambers was as proud of her handsome little hero as he was fond of his dashing red-haired beauty. I never met Bat at that time, but I had known Annie both in Leavenworth and Ellsworth. She was as fine a girl as ever set in a frontier town by the ears, and she was better educated than most women of her kind.

Sergeant King, one of the most notorious bullies and gunfighters in the army, wanted to dance with Annie one night and because she refused he pulled his six-shooter and shot her in the breast. Even as she fell, dying, into Bat's arms the latter jerked his gun on the soldier and shot him dead, but not before King had pumped lead into Bat's groin.[2]

That was one of the killings for which Bat Masterson has been held up by some ignorant writers as a shocking example of ferocity and lawlessness. But of the many men he killed there was not one who was not in the wrong, and not one who did not start in with the best of the fight. Shocking as it may seem to civilized souls, we had our crude code of honor on the frontier. When I speak of a fair fighter I mean a man who will not take his enemy at a disadvantage. Such a man is Bat Masterson.

Bat was acquited, of course, and soon afterward came over to Dodge City, where I had just been installed as city marshal.[3]

Bat Masterson in his later years as a gambler in Denver, Colorado.

His fame as the hero of 'dobe Walls and the slayer of Sergeant King had preceded Bat to Dodge, and he attracted no end of respectful attention as he limped from one gambling house to another, still pale and weak from the effect of King's bullet. He was somewhat of a dandy in those days, but before all else he was a man. Not that his physique entitled him to attention beyond other men, for in his case nature had packed a big consignment of dynamic energy into a small compass and corded it up tight. But there was something in the way his bullet-shaped head was mounted on his square shoulders, something in the grain of his crisp, wiry hair, something in the tilt of his short nose that bespoke an animal courage such as not every man is endowed withal.

Mere animal courage has made many a man a brute and an assassin, but Bat Masterson had a wealth of saving graces which shone from the honest fullness of his face. I have already spoken of his eyes. They were well-nigh unendurable in conflict —so bold, so bright, so unmitigable was their gaze; but in moments of peace they danced with mischief, with generosity, with affection. A small and carefully nurtured coal-black mustache half hid a mouth which was readier to soften in mirth than to harden in anger, and the stubborn chin beneath was cleft with the dimple that physiognomists interpret as the symbol of a kindly heart.

In moving from Wichita to take the Marshalship of Dodge City at my own salary I had stipulated that I should have the appointment of my own police force. A fair judge of manhood as I esteemed myself, what wonder that I should have fastened hungry official eyes upon the hero of 'dobe Walls?

"Bat," said I, "will you join the force?"

"I'd like it first rate," he replied.

"Then throw away that cane and get to work," I said.[4]

And forthwith Bat was sworn in to protect the peace.

During the summer that he served with me——before he

ran for sheriff[5] and was elected——stirring events came to pass in Dodge City. And like the Arizona feud of which I have already written, they all arose out of one small incident. That incident was the killing of "The Nightingale."[6]

One night a Texas desperado named Kenedy was diverting himself at a dance hall by flourishing his six-shooter. Mayor Kelly happened to be there, and as there was no officer present to restrain the Texan he took it upon himself to interfere.

"You'd better give them guns to the bartender, my boy," he said kindly, "or some of my men will arrest ye."

Kenedy resented the suggestion and there was a dispute, but there was no word or thought of killing at that time. The Mayor's remonstrance rankled in Kenedy's mind, however, and at 2 o'clock in the morning he started out to kill the Chief Executive.

Mounting his horse, so as to be in readiness for flight, the Texan rode down to the house where Kelly lived. The room where the Mayor and his wife slept opened on to the street, and Kenedy knew the direction in which the bed lay at the opposite end of the room. On the other side of a slender partition was another bed, occupied by Willett and his wife. Willett was a clerk for a neighboring grocer; his wife was a vaudeville woman of varied experiences on the frontier, and so sweet a singer that she was called "The Nightingale." Ask any man who knew Deadwood or Dodge in its prime to tell you how she sang "Killiarney."

And so, making a careful estimation of the elevation of the Mayor's bed, Kenedy began to empty his Winchester through the panels of the door. He calculated well, for two bullets went through the down comforter under which the Kellys slumbered. Nearly all the shots penetrated the partition behind their bed.

About that time Willett half awoke and turned over on his side, throwing his arm around his wife. At his touch her body fluttered like that of a wounded bird, and something bubbled in her throat. Willett was wide awake in an instant——he did not know why. His hand touched something wet upon her breast and he asked her what it was, but there was no reply. Willett jumped out of bed and lit a match. It was blood upon his hand. It was blood upon the woman's breast. A bullet had torn its way clear through her body. The Nightingale was dead.

Wyatt Tells of Bat Masterson   135

Poor Willett ran over to me and I pulled on my clothes in a hurry. The only house where there was a light was the Long Branch Saloon, so I went in there for information. Kenedy was there, sitting on a monte table, swinging his legs.

"Was he here when the shots were fired?" I whispered to the bartender.

"For God's sake don't say anything here," was the reply. "Come into the back room and I'll tell you all about it."

"Kenedy's the man," he continued excitedly, when we had retired out of earshot. "He left here with another man just before the shooting and immediately afterward he came in the back way and took a big drink of whiskey."

I ran back to the bar, but Kenedy had gone.

Bat joined me just then. He had been down to the house and the Mayor had told him all about the trouble in the dance hall. In searching the town for Kenedy we ran across the man in whose company he had left the saloon, and this fellow more than confirmed our suspicions of the Texan's guilt. Moreover, he led us to the alley where the murderer had tied his horse, and from there we picked up a clear trail leading out of the city.

At daylight Bat, Bill Tilghman and I started out on the trail, taking this man along with us. For two days we followed it across the prairie toward the Texas border, and then a heavy rainstorm came up and swept away all vestige of a hoof print.

At a distance of nearly 100 miles from Dodge we made a circuit of fifteen miles in order to get to a ranch for the night.

"Some of these here Texans are going home pretty early ain't they?" was the ranchman's greeting. "Kenedy was here yesterday afternoon, and he seemed in a hurry too."

Thus we picked up another trail, only to lose it again next day, when we were overtaken by more rain. In this predicament we made for a ranch twenty miles further on and reached the place at 3 o'clock in the afternoon. Our horses were fagged out, so we turned them out to grass and prepared to rest ourselves. After a while we caught sight of a horseman four or five miles away across the prairie, evidently making for the ranch. We watched him with idle curiosity and when he came within a couple of miles of us, Bat said with conviction: "That's Kenedy, I know him by the way he rides, and besides, I know his horse." And when the stranger had arrived within a mile of the ranch we all knew that Bat, who had the eye of a hawk, was right.

Our horses were scattered over the pasture and it was too late to attempt to capture them. We agreed that it would be unwise to wait until Kenedy should get too close, least he should recognize our horses and wheel in his tracks. So we ambushed ourselves behind a heap of earth that had been thrown up from a new wall, first agreeing that if he should scent danger and turn to make a run for it I should kill the horse and Bat attend to the man.

When he came within seventy-five yards of us we rose up and called him to halt. He whipped out his gun, firing at us as he wheeled his horse. True to our agreement I shot the horse, which dropped just as Bat landed a bullet in Kenedy's shoulder.

Well, we took away his six-shooters and his Winchester, hired a team and drove him back to Dodge. But the brute was never convicted. He was a son of a multi-millionaire cattleman by a Mexican mother, and his father's money procured him endless delays, and finally an acquittal.

But the incidents connected with the wounding and capture of Kenedy, for the murder of the Nightingale deepened the hatred bestowed upon Bat Masterson and myself by the Texan rustlers from whose violence we tried to protect the citizens of Dodge. Dodge had become the center of the cattle trade then and the periodic incursions of cowboys, whose chief ambition was to be able to go back to Texas and boast of having "killed an of'cer" were the curse of the community. The townspeople hated the Texans, and the Texans despised the townspeople. In the vernacular of the feud the Southerners were "longhorns," and the Northerners "shorthorns."

It was after Bat Masterson had been returned as sheriff that I paid the visit to Mexico, during which I first met Doc Holliday and his Big-Nose Kate, as told in a previous story. During my absence Ed Masterson, Bat's elder brother, acted as my deputy. A crowd of cowboys started shooting in the Birdcage dance hall one night and Ed went over to see about it. He disarmed them all and made them pile their guns behind the bar. Then he returned across the deadline——the avenue formed by the railroad tracks, which divided the decent from the disreputable part of the town. Not long afterward, however, the cowboys recovered their six-shooters and began firing again. Ed went back to restore order and tried to disarm the first cowboy he encountered. The two men were scuffling for possession of the gun, when another cowboy fired at Ed Masterson and killed him.

Just at that moment Bat Masterson had appeared, attracted by the shooting. He saw his brother fall and with a quick drop killed the man who had fired the shot. The rest began to run away shooting and Bat winged the man with whom Ed had been scuffling. He died a few days later, while they were taking him back to Texas.[7]

Thus was perpetrated another of the so-called atrocities with which the hero of 'dobe Walls was to be reproached in after years by writers whose knowledge of the frontier was derived from Bowery melodramas.

In view of the bloody complications closing in on my narrative it is high time that I introduce Bob Wright,[8] the deus-ex-machina of much of the violent work that followed. Bob Wright was a tower of strength to the Texas faction. He had lived in their country and he depended on their patronage for the prosperity of his store, which was one of the largest in the city. He was a legislator, too——a duly elected representative from the county.

Bob Wright sought to interfere with me one night because I was taking one ill-behaved cattleman, who happened to be worth some millions of dollars, to the calaboose. My prisoner had tried to kill an inoffensive Dutch fiddler for not playing his favorite tune often enough to please him. The cattleman appealed to Wright, and Wright threatened to have me put off the city force if I persisted in the arrest. The upshot of it was that I threw Wright into the calaboose to keep his friend company for the night. It was soon after that incident that the Texans began to hatch plots to kill me by foul means or fair——preferably the former.[9]

The first attempt fell to the lot of a desperado named Hoyt, who was no 'prentice in the art of assassination. I was standing on the sidewalk outside a saloon one bright moonlight night, talking to Eddie Foy, who was leaning against the doorway, when Hoyt came riding down the street on a white horse. I noticed that he had his right hand by his side but did not suspect anything until he came within ten steps of where I was standing. Then he threw his gun over like lightening and took a shot at me.

Jim Masterson, Bat's brother, served as a deputy sheriff under Bat.

EARLE 80

By the time he was on a level with me had taken another shot, but both missed.

I ran out, intending to pull him off his horse, and failing that, I tried to grab his horse's tail as it passed me, and as Hoyt dug in his spurs he wheeled in his saddle and fired at me again. With that I crouched down in the middle of the road for a steady aim and emptied my gun after him as he tore down the road. I saw him disappear over the bridge that spanned the Arkansas river, and made sure I had missed him. But five minutes later, when I was telling the story to Bat Masterson and a crowd of citizens, the white horse came galloping back, mounted by a boy, who told us that its rider was lying badly shot just beyond the bridge. Half suspecting an ambush, Bat and I took shotguns and went back with the boy. There, sure enough, was Hoyt, full of lead and remorse, and groaning most dolefully. Two or three days later he died. [10]

This episode was not without its humorous side, for to this day, Eddie Foy, the comedian, is fond of telling how, at the first shot, he threw himself under a monte table and stayed there till the shooting was over.

And so Clay Allison came to town, and for a whole day behaved like a veritable chesterfield. But the next morning one of my policemen woke me up to tell me that the bad man from Colorado was loaded up with a pair of six-shooters and a mouth full of threats. Straightaway I put my guns on and went down the street with Bat Masterson. Now, Bat had a shotgun in the District Attorney's office, which was behind a drugstore just opposite Wright's store. He thought the weapon might come in handy in case of trouble, so he skipped across the street to get it. But not caring to be seen with such a weapon before there was any occasion for it, he stayed over there, talking to some people outside the drugstore, while I went into Webster's Saloon looking for Allison. I saw at a glance that my man wasn't there, and had just reached the sidewalk to turn into the Long Branch, next door, when I met him face to face. We greeted each other with caution thinly veiled by ---, and as we spoke backed carelessly up against the wall, I on the right. There we stood, measuring each other with sideway glances. An onlooker across the street might have thought we were old friends.

"So," said Allison truculently, "you're the man that killed my friend Hoyt."

"Yes, I guess I'm the man you're looking for," said I.

His right hand was stealing round to his pistol pocket, but I made no move. Only I watched him narrowly. With my own right hand I had a firm grip on my six-shooter, and with my left I was ready to grab Allison's gun the moment he jerked it out. He studied the situation in all its bearings for the space of a second or two. I saw the change in his face.

"I guess I'll go round the corner," he said abruptly.

"I guess you'd better," I replied.

And he went. [11]

In the meantime ten or a dozen of the worst Texans in town were laying low in Bob Wright's Store, with their Winchesters, ready to cover Allison's retreat out of town, or help him in the killing, if necessary. From where he had stationed himself Bat Masterson could see them, but I did not know they were there.

Clay Allison of Colorado was one of the dangerous gunfighters who visited Dodge City during the days of Wyatt and Masterson.

After the encounter with Allison I moved up the street and would have passed Bob Wright's door had not Bat, from across the street signaled to me to keep out of range. A moment later Allison, who had mounted his horse, rode out in front of Webster's and called to me.

"Come over here, Wyatt," he said, "I want to talk to you."

"I can hear you all right here," I replied. "I think you came here to make a fight with me, and if you did you can have it right now."

Several friends of mine wanted me to take a shotgun, but I thought I could kill him all right with a six-shooter. At that moment Bob Wright came running down the street to urge Allison to go out of town. He had experienced a sudden change of heart because Bat had crossed over to him with these portentous words: "If this fight comes up, Wright, you're the first man I'm going to kill." Allison listened to the legislator's entreaties with a scowl.

"Well I don't like you any too well," he said, "there were alot of your friends to be here this morning to help me out, but I don't see them round now."

"Earp, he continued, turning to me and raising his voice. "I believe you're a pretty good man from what I've seen of you. Do you know that these coyotes sent for me to make a fight with you and kill you? Well, I'm going to ride out of town, and I wish you good luck."

And so Clay Allison made his exit. Ten days later he re-appeared within a mile of town and sent a messenger asking my permission to come into Dodge and attend to some business regarding his cattle. I sent him word that he was welcome to come so long as he behaved himself. He availed himself of the offer, and for two weeks he behaved like an exemplary citizen. It was a fourteen day wonder, for Allison had never in his life before conducted himself like a Christian. Indeed, it had been his practice to force every saloon and bank other than those he patronized to close up during such time as he honored a frontier town with a visit.

A year or so later Allison came to an ignominious end by falling off a wagon and breaking his neck.

It was a day or two after my bloodless encounter with the famous Colorado fighter that Wright came to me with the olive branch, made a clean break of the Hoyt and Allison conspiracies, and offered me his friendship in return for my protection from his erstwhile friends, the Texans.

Even the Allison adventure was topped off with an epilogue of a grim humorous kind, which I cannot forbear telling. Bat Masterson was speculating on the havoc his shotgun would have wreaked the ranks of the cowboys if he had enjoyed a chance to use it that morning, and for the sake of a change of air and a little target practice he and I rode out of town, upended a broad plank and began firing at it. First of all Bat fired both barrels of his shotgun, which was loaded just as he had picked it up in the District Attorney's office when I was looking for Allison.

Walking up to the board he found to his dismay that the gun had been loaded not with buckshot as he thought, but with the finest of birdshot. Somebody, he learned afterwards, had borrowed the gun for a day's sport, and had left it loaded on returning it to its place.

"It would have been just the same," grumbled Bat, "if a good man's life had depended on that charge in that gun."

And now for the last, but not the least dramatic episode by which Bat's memory and mine are linked with Dodge City of what I can't help thinking a decadent if more decorous era.

As the town grew civilized Bat Masterson and I drifted to Tombstone, Jim Masterson, another of Bat's brothers, remained in Dodge, a partner with Updegraff and Peacock in the possession of a saloon and gambling house. Jim had a dispute with his partners about the division of profits,[12] and three or four of their creatures jumped on him. He escaped to his room with the intention of getting a gun and they surrounded the place keeping him prisoner a whole day. Some of his friends telegraphed for Bat, and he traveled the 1,500 miles to make a fight with his brother's enemies.

He arrived in Dodge at 9 o'clock, one morning, and had hardly stepped from the train when the other faction, who knew of his coming, started across the deadline to meet him. When they got within fifty yards of him they gave him a shot or two by way of welcome, and he returned the fire with such effect as to inflict a mortal wound on Updegraff. [13]

Thereupon Mayor Webster appeared with a double-barreled shotgun and arrested Bat, who was afterwards fined $10 and ordered to leave Dodge for the rest of his life. You see, Dodge had become so civilized that it had no further use for the men who had been its best protectors in the days of the Texas Terror.

It was not long after Bat's banishment that this very Webster, the mayor, fell foul of another frontiersman——no less redoubtable a gambler and gunfighter than Luke Short. Luke and a man named Harris kept a gambling house next door to one kept by the Mayor, and as Luke was well known in Texas and all over the frontier they enjoyed most of the patronage. In order to harass his rivals the Mayor had an ordinance passed denying women free access to the saloons [14] a perogative which they had heretofore enjoyed in Dodge. Moreover, he secured a piano to add to the attractions of his own place and imported a professor to play it.

Short and Harris promptly furnished themselves with a handsome piano and hired two girls to play and sing. Webster ordered a policeman to arrest these two girls, and they were taken to the calaboose. Luke went over to bail them out, but the policeman refused to accept his bonds. In the argument that ensued the policeman fired at Luke and Luke shot the policeman in the leg. [15]

Thereupon Webster organized a shotgun brigade among his friends, and in the morning they marched Luke down to the depot, bundled him on board a train, and warned him never again to return to Dodge City. Apart from the ignominy of the thing and the natural desire to get square with his enemy, this was a serious matter for Luke, who had been dragged away from a profitable business in the city. So he telegraphed to Bat Masterson, and the pair of them, inspired by mutual friendship and a common grievance, tried to devise measures by which they could force the authorities of Dodge to receive them with the distinguished consideration which they conceived to be their due. Among other measures, they laid their grievance before the Governor of the State, who expressed his entire sympathy with them, and advised them to fight their way into the city if necessary. [16]

In this extremity, they resorted to get my assistance, and Bat jumped on a train for Silverton, Colorado, where I was living at the time. (It should be understood that all this happened subsequent to the vendetta which resulted in my leaving Arizona).

Well, I was only too ready for anything with a spice of adventure in it, and especially for a chance to help two old friends. In particular I was indignant at the ingratitude with which Bat Masterson had been served by the city he had protected so well in its darkest hours. So I gathered around me a company of rough diamonds who had seen me through many a tough fight in Arizona, and started for Dodge City. Bat stopped off at Trinidad, for it was agreed that I and my merry men should go alone to make terms with the enemy. Luke Short was at Wichita.

Our train got to Dodge at 10 o'clock in the morning and we marched up the street to Luke's Saloon. I with my Wells-Fargo shotgun and my men with their Winchesters. Body of

W. B. Bat Masterson
as he appeared as
the sheriff of Ford
County, Kansas,
in 1877.

Bacchua! No wonder Dodge City rubbed its eyes. There was Millsap, there was Shotgun Collins, there was Shoot-Your-Eye-Out Jack who wore his hair down to his waist, and there was Crooked-Mouth Green, whose features had been so mutilated by a bullet that his mouth extended round to the back of his head. Faithful followers and quick fighters, everyone one of 'em.[17]

We met the District Attorney going up the street and his face wore a careworn, "come ye in peace now or come ye in war" look as he exclaimed: "My God Wyatt! Who are these people you've got with you?"

"Oh," said I, carelessly, "they're just some bushwackers I've brought over from Colorado to straighten you people out."

"In whose interest?" he asked.

"Luke Short's and Bat Masterson's," I replied.

A few paces further on I met Mayor Webster, who shook hands with me with an air of cordiality that the yellowish pallor of his cheeks belied. We all filed into Luke's saloon and there we were sworn in as deputies by Prairie Dog Dave, the constable, who was with us blood and bones, as all the good people in town were. Indeed, the city was sick of the Webster reign of terror and glad to see a way out of it, and I soon had a following of a hundred or more fighters ready to do my bidding. It was no mean advantage to be deputized by Prairie Dog Dave, for that enabled us to carry our arms without violating the law concerning which Dodge had become so sensitive.

The town council convened a hurried meeting and sent for me to ask my intentions. I told them that I wanted Luke Short and Bat Masterson to return to Dodge at their pleasure. I added that if this were accomplished peacefully I would be so much better pleased but that if necessary I was prepared to fight for my demands. In reply they offered to compromise. They would permit Luke to return for ten days to wind up his business. Bat Masterson they would not permit to enter the town. To this proposition I made no reply, but walked out of the council room. Soon afterward they sent for me again, and I again assured them that there could be no compromise——that Luke and Bat must be free to live in Dodge as long as they wanted to, provided they obeyed the laws.

Before the council had made any decision I wired to Luke Short to meet me at Kingsley, thirty miles away. I had an idea he might decide to return with me, so I gave orders to my followers to post themselves in front of Wright's and at other strategic points in case of disturbance. Luke and I dined together at Kingsley and, as I had anticipated, he resolved to come back with me. But we agreed that we would let the other fellows begin the fighting.

Luke and I jumped off the rear platform of the sleeper as the train slowed up, each with a double-barreled shotgun in readiness and advanced up the street, fully expecting to make a stiff fight for it. But the enemy didn't appear. That night I telegraphed to Bat, telling him to come on the next train. He arrived in the morning and had no sooner alighted than a deputy sheriff demanded his shotgun, but I would not let him give it up.

I had hard work to persuade Bat to go into Webster's and shake hands with the Mayor, but he consented at last and the trouble was over in a few minutes. We had conquered Dodge City without firing a shot. It was a great moral victory, for Bat and Luke were unmolested from that time forth. Not that Bat stayed long to enjoy the fruits of his vindication, for he was then City Marshal of Trinidad.

Among other manifestations of exuberance at the successful issue of our invasion the citizens dubbed us "the Dodge City Peace Commission" and had us photographed in a group, which is hereby reproduced. Crooked-Mouth Green and my other picturesque henchmen did not figure in this group, as they felt sensitive about submitting their physiognomies to the fierce light of frontier history, which is really a pity.

As everybody knows Bat Masterson has now for many years been identified with Denver, where he is appreciated at his true worth. His association with the prize ring and other forms of sport, all over the country, has brought his name prominently before a younger and more effete generation. And he has fallen into flesh. But to me he will always be Bat Masterson, the quick fighter, the square gambler, the staunch friend and generous foe—the fastest of my frontier friends.

Wyatt S. Earp.

HISTORICAL NOTES AND EDITORIAL COMMENTS

1. The story of Adobe Walls as recorded here is only partially correct. It was not five scouts against five hundred Indians, but thirty-four hunters against a very large group of determined savages. General Nelson A. Miles did not gather his detachment of scouts until later. Wyatt Earp was undoubtedly telling the story from memory, as it was related to him by Bat Masterson while the two were in Dodge City.

In the first place "Adobe Walls" was a settlement consisting of two stores, a blacksmith shop, and a saloon; it was not a single adobe ruin as Earp describes it here. The buildings were not deserted, but were being used as a frontier outpost for the convenience of buffalo hunters and isolated settlers in the Texas Panhandle. According to John Coulter, a reporter for the Leavenworth *Times* (November 17, 1877), the stores were those of Charles Rath & Co., and Leonard and Myers; the blacksmith shop belonged to Tom Kief, and the saloon was kept by James Hanrahan. The attack took place on June 27, 1874, and was carried out by a group of two to five hundred Indians. The Leavenworth *Daily Commercial* printed a list of thirty-four men, including William Dixon and Bat Masterson, who repulsed the attack at Adobe Walls.

This battle was a part of a general Indian outbreak which resulted in the formation of an expedition under the command of General Nelson A. Miles about August 1, 1874. General Miles reported the following about the fight at Adobe Walls in his memoirs, *Personal Recollections of General Nelson A. Miles*, pp. 160-61.

> One of the first attacks in force was upon those whom they hated most——the buffalo hunters. A large camp of these hunters located at what was known as Adobe Walls, a trading post on the Canadian River in the Panhandle of Texas, and this the Indians attempted to capture by surprise. It was their intention to annihilate the whole band of hunters at the first dash. In the latter part of June, two hundred warriors made a descent upon the camp, but unfortunately for them the day happened to be Sunday, when the buffalo hunters were all gathered for a day of rest and recreation and were therefore all together in full strength. The Indians made the attack suddenly and in a most determined manner. The hunters being most expert in the use of the rifle and accustomed to accurate shooting, and fighting from behind the thick protecting walls of the building, were cool and careful in their aim and played sad havoc with the charging Indians. They had shown remarkable courage, frequently pushing right up to the stockade and fighting almost hand to hand trying to break down the doors. The fight was kept up for several hours, and then for three days they maintained a siege. It was an old-fashioned fight of frontiersmen against rude warriors, in which the latter were no match for the skilled riflemen.
> . . . Troops arrived there some days after the siege had been raised, and the scene which met their gaze told a story of the depravity of these men, physically brave and generous where Indians are not concerned, which needs no comment from me. After stating the number of the dead buried by the Indians, the account as transmitted to the eastern press, gravely adds, "Twelve more were left where they fell, and the heads of these twelve men were found adorning the gateposts of the hunters' corral."

2. The killing of Sergeant Melvin A. King by Bat Masterson is difficult to document because few, if any contemporary records are available covering Bat's life from March, 1875, through the spring of 1877. The Earp story printed here was evidently related to him by Masterson.

There is a basis in fact for the story, however, since the February 11, 1876, *Frontier Echo*, a Jacksboro, Texas, newspaper reported the following: *Telegraphic News:* "King of H Company, 4th Cavalry and a woman, Molly Braman, killed at San Antonio by a citizen."

Also, the muster roll of Company H, Fourth Cavalry, indicates that King died at a cantonment on Sweetwater Creek, Texas, January 25, 1876, from a pistol wound not received in the line of duty. See, Nyle H. Miller and Joseph W. Snell, *Why the West Was Wild*, p. 322.

There are minor differences in the above citations in regards to the place and date of Sergeant King's death; and the story is further complicated by Wyatt Earp giving the girl's name as Annie Chambers instead of Molly Braman. Prostitutes, however, used various names on the frontier.

3. See annotation No. 4, Chapter 1.

Wyatt only attained the rank of assistant marshal on the Dodge City police force.

4. Wyatt Earp was again giving himself "the best of it" by claiming that he hired Bat Masterson to work on the Dodge City police force. Hiring policemen was the job of the city council, which was usually following the recommendation of the Marshal (in this case, Lawrence E. Deger). It then follows that Bat did not work all summer for Earp.

Masterson was a special policeman for Dodge City for about ten days during September of 1877, at least he was paid for ten days. Wyatt Earp was on his Texas trip at this time and did not return to Dodge until shortly after Edward Masterson was killed. Any cooperation between Bat Masterson and Wyatt Earp as lawmen came after Bat was appointed undersheriff by Charles E. Bassett, or Bat, himself, had been elected Sheriff of Ford County.

5. Wyatt had his timing wrong on the killing of "the Nightingale." Bat was elected sheriff of Ford County November 6, 1877, and began serving January 14, 1878. "The Nightingale," Dora Hand, alias Fannie Keenan, was killed October 4, 1878. Bat Masterson was already sheriff of Ford County when the killing took place.

6. No killing in Dodge City history angered the citizenry of the camp more than the "accidental" shooting of "the Nightingale," with the exception, perhaps, of the murder of City Marshal Ed Masterson. The love the people bestowed upon this "lady of the night" was aptly illustrated by the large throng that attended her funeral, and as one paper reported, "Not a single eye was dry as the ceremony ended."

Her murder was the result of an assassination attempt by James "Spike" Kenedy on the life of James H. Kelley, Dodge City's mayor. The young Texan, the son of a wealthy cattleman, Miflin Kenedy, part owner of the huge King Ranch in Texas, held a grudge against the mayor and was seeking revenge. Mayor Kelley had disarmed the "cocky" young man for flourishing his six-shooter in a dangerous manner in the bar.

Young Kenedy's mode of operation was both simple and effective: later that night he rode past the mayor's house and emptied his revolver through a window into what he believed to be Kelley's bed. Confident that revenge had been served, he returned to the saloon to continue his drinking.

The story given by contemporary newspapers differs in minor respects from Wyatt Earp's version. It may never be known, at this late date, what actually happened in exact detail.

Wyatt Earp has Mrs. Willett (Dora Hand, alias Fannie Keenan) sleeping in the back room of Mayor James H. Kelley's house with her husband, Willett, a clerk of a local grocery store. The mayor's bed in the front room was empty. One of Kenedy's shots penetrated the thin partition and killed Mrs. Willett instantly. Earp gave Kenedy's motive for the shooting as revenge for a quarrel that occurred earlier in the evening with the mayor.

Newspaper accounts of the incident, the Dodge City *Times*, October 5, 1878; *Ford County Globe*, October 8, 1878; and the St. Louis *Daily Journal*, October 11, 1878; reported that another woman, Miss Fannie Garretson, was sleeping in Mayor Kelley's bed. The newspapers disclosed the fact that the mayor was in the hospital in Fort Dodge taking treatment. Differing again from Wyatt's version of the tale, the papers claimed it was an old grudge that dated back several days which caused the trouble.

Again, the various names attributed to "the Nightingale," Dora Hand, Mrs. Theodore Hand, Fannie Keenan, and Mrs. Willett, cause confusion but perhaps she went by all of these names at various times.

One of the better accounts of this incident is given in Harry Sinclair Drago's book *Wild, Wooly & Wicked*, pp. 313-316. It differs from Earp's story in that Kenedy plotted his revenge for several days. First he determined the mayor's habits, and where he slept. Then he left for Kansas City by stage and bought the fastest horse available. Forty-eight days after his fight with Kelley, Kenedy rode back into Dodge, past the house of the mayor, firing several shots, aiming, he hoped, into the mayor's bed. Sure of his success, Kenedy headed for the safety of Texas immediately. However, during the time Kenedy was away from Dodge, Kelley had become ill and was in the hospital in Fort Dodge. His house had been rented to Fannie Keenan and Fannie Garretson. The former was sleeping in the back room, and the latter was sleeping in the front room in the mayor's bed. While both women were well-liked by Dodge City's populace, their reputations were questionable at best.

When he was captured, "Spike" Kenedy was astonished to learn that he would be charged with the death of Fannie Keenan, the popular entertainer, rather than Mayor Kelley.

7. See annotation No. 7, Chapter 1. Bat did not avenge his brother's death by shooting his killers. Ed, himself, did this before he died.

8. It was quite evident that Wyatt Earp and Bob Wright did not "hit it off." Wright was, perhaps, the biggest businessman in Dodge City, and as such was friendly with the Texans who spent a great deal of money in town. The economics of the problem clearly shows why Bob Wright favored the drovers over any of Dodge City's institutions: police force, city council, or administration. As to the question of Earp throwing Wright in jail historians are divided. Pro-Earp writers say he did; those who dislike Earp claim he did not. The Dodge City newspapers give few references which indicate a general dislike for Texans by local residents. It is probable that Texans and their money were considered a necessary evil.

The city fathers soon realized that a large and tough police force was needed to control the large and potentially dangerous group of celebrating cowboys. Since Dodge City's budget was limited, tough officers were evidently hired as an alternative to size. Men of the caliber of Wyatt Earp, the Masterson brothers, Charles Bassett, and William Tilghman, were invaluable, although they were seldom paid more than a hundred dollars a month. Much to the credit of the Ford County and Dodge City lawmen, they kept

The Dodge City Peace Commission who joined together to help their friend, Luke Short, in Dodge City. Left to right, top row: William H. Harris, Luke Short, Bat Masterson. Bottom row: Charley Bassett, Wyatt Earp, McLean and Neal Brown. (Dallas Public Library).

law and order with relatively little shooting and killing. Harry Sinclair Drago in his book, *Wild, Woolly, & Wicked*, p. 312, described the situation in the following manner: "There was a lot of killing in Dodge, but not by its peace officers."

9. There is no evidence of a serious attempt on Wyatt Earp's life while he was in Dodge City. Although he did jail a number of drovers, he generally got along with both the owners and the drovers. If the Texans had wanted to kill him, it would have been a simple task. A shot from ambush on a dark night would have been all that was necessary and such a job could have been bought for under a hundred dollars.

10. Wyatt Earp's version of the killing of George Hoy (Hoyt) was repeated by Bat Masterson on a number of occasions, and has found its way into the literature of the Kansas cow towns. Contemporary newspapers, however, provide more precise details of the incident. The *Times* of July 27, 1878, described the killing of George Hoyt in this manner:

BULLETS IN THE AIR
Music from the Festive Revolver
Twenty Shots Fired and Only One Man Wounded.

Yesterday morning about 3 o'clock this peaceful suburban city was thrown into unusual excitement, and the turmoil was all caused by a rantankerous cowboy who started the mischief by a too free use of his little revolver...

... It seems that three or four herders were paying their respects to the city and its institutions, and as was usually their custom, remained until 3 o'clock in the morning, when they prepared to return to their camps. They buckled on their revolvers, which they were not allowed to wear around town, and mounted their horses, when all at once one of them conceived the idea to finish the night's revelry and give the natives due warning of his departure, he must do some shooting, and forthwith he commenced to bang away, one of the bullets whizzing into a dance hall nearby, causing no little commotion among the participants in the "dreamy Waltz" and quadrille. Policemen Earp and Masterson [James Masterson] made a raid on the shootists who gave them two or three volleys, but fortunately without effect. The policeman returned the fire and followed the herders with the intention of arresting them. The firing became general, and some rooster who did not exactly understand the situation, perched himself in the window of the dance hall and indulged in a promiscuous shot all by himself... A few yards from the bridge one of the herders fell from his horse from weakness caused by a wound in the arm he had received during the fracas... The wounded man was properly cared for and his wound, which proved to be a bad one, was dressed by Dr. McCarty. His name is George Hoy [Hoyt].

Another account of the Hoyt affair was written in the *Ford County Globe* of July 30, 1878. Also on August 27, 1878, the *Globe* announced that George Hoyt the young Texan "who was wounded some weeks since in the midnight scrimmage, died from the effects of his wound." This was almost a month after he had been shot by an unknown person. The *Globe* also stated that although he was under $1,500 bond for aiding in the rounding up of cattle that someone else claimed (rustling), he was in no wise a criminal and probably would have been released at the next term of the District Court.

11. In spite of Earp's claim to having faced down Clay Allison in Dodge City, no newspaper story or other evidence has been found to document the act. The reverse is also true, there is no way to prove that Allison did not have a confrontation with Earp and then backed down. In fact, there is little mention of Clay Allison in available Dodge City publications, and the newspaper files of the Kansas Historical Society are fairly complete.

The *Ford County Globe* for August 6, 1878, mentions: "Clay Allison, one of the Allison brothers, from the Cimarron, south of Las Animas, Colorado, stopped off at Dodge last week on his way home from Saint Louis. We are glad to say that Clay has about recovered from the effects of the East St. Louis scrimmage." In their excellent book, *Why the West Was Wild*, Nyle H. Miller and Joseph W. Snell, pp. 25-26, state that the Saint Louis scrimmage may be the incident reported in the St. Louis *Missouri Republican* for July 25, 1878. This paper described a "lively encounter between Alexander Kessinger and a Texas drover "who gives his name as Allison." Demonstrating that Allison could be whipped. Kessinger knocked Allison down and gave him a fearful beating until the Texan cried for quarter. A year and a half later, on February 26, 1880, Allison sent a card to the *Globe* giving his version of the difficulty: "I do not claim to be a prize fighter, but as an evidence of the correct result of this fight I will only say that I was somewhat hurt but did not squeal, as did my three opponents." It has never been determined if he was beaten by one man or three men.

Clay Allison is mentioned in the *Ford County Globe* on September 10, 1878, reporting that he had visited Dodge City on September 5. The *Globe* also makes note of him on August 17, 1880, as having come up "from the Pan Handle Sunday." The *Globe Livestock Journal* for July 26, 1887, printed Clay Allison's obituary stating that he had fallen from a wagon and the wheel passed over his head.

If there was a showdown between Earp and Allison, it would have occurred on one of the first two trips Allison made to Dodge because Earp left for Tombstone early in September of 1879. It is also possible that his visits to Dodge were not always noted by the papers. Charley Siringo, the cowboy detective, related a Clay Allison story which never appeared in any of the papers.

12. Al Updegraff stated in a letter printed in the May 10, 1881, *Ford County Globe* that the trouble started when James Masterson tried to protect a friend of his who had robbed a woman of $80. (She was probably a girl friend of Al Updegraff.) Masterson tried to get Updegraff to get his girl friend to drop the charges. When he refused to do so, Masterson fired him. A. J. Peacock, Masterson's saloon partner, insisted that the bartender remain on the job. This situation resulted in a fight between Al Updegraff and James Masterson in which Masterson was the loser. It was then that James wired Bat for help.

13. Al Updegraff was only wounded, dying almost a year later of pneumonia.

14. No one questioned that the real profession of these women was prostitution. It was the partiality with which the new ordinances against prostitution and vagrancy were enforced that caused the trouble. On May 1, 1883, the *Globe* stated: "It was claimed by the properietors [Short and Harris] that partiality was shown in arresting women in their house when two were allowed to remain in A. B. Webster's saloon."

15. Most sources say neither man was wounded. The *Globe* of May 1, 1883, reports that "Luke Short and L. C. Hartman met upon the street and paid their respective compliments to each other by exchanging shots, fortunately no one was hurt."

16. In answer to telegrams from Sheriff Hinkle, Robert M. Wright, and J. R. Hardesty, the Governor sent the following letter to the sheriff, indicating his distress at the unlawful conditions prevailing in Dodge City and referring to the mob headed by the mayor on several occasions:

The accounts of the way things have been going on there are simply monstrous, and it requires that the disgrace that is being brought upon Dodge City, and the State of Kansas, by the conduct that is represented to have occurred there, should be wiped out. Your dispatch to me presents an extraordinary state of affairs, one that is outrageous upon its face. You tell me that the mayor has compelled several parties to leave town for refusing to comply with the ordinances. Such a statement as that if true, simply shows that the mayor is unfit for his place, that he does not do his duty, and instead of occupying the position of peacemaker, the man whose duty it is to see that the ordinances are enforced by legal processes in the courts, starts out to head a mob to drive people away from their homes and their business. . .

17. The strategy of the Short-Harris-Masterson faction in the Dodge City War was now apparent. Numerous well-known gunfighters and hard cases, who were well-armed, would move into Dodge City and enforce their will by either "war," or the threat of "war." In any case, their war cry was, "let the other side start the shooting." The Kansas City *Journal*, May 15, 1883, carried the following:

Yesterday a new man arrived on the scene who is destined to play a part in a great tragedy. This man is Bat Masterson, ex-sheriff of Ford County, and one of the most dangerous men the West has ever produced. A few years ago he incurred the enmity of the same men who drove Short away, and he was exiled upon the pain of death if he returned

Front Street of Dodge City,
Kansas, when it was walked
by Masterson and Earp.
(Kansas Historical Society).

[this was for the wounding of Al Updegraff on the streets of Dodge City in 1881]. His presence in Kansas City means just one thing, and that he is going to visit Dodge City. Masterson precedes by twenty-four hours a few other pleasant gentlemen who are on their way to the tea party at Dodge. One of them is Wyatt Earp, the famous marshal of Dodge, another is Joe Lowe, otherwise known as "Rowdy Joe," and still another is "Shotgun Collins," worse than all is another ex-citizen and officer of Dodge, the famous Doc Halliday [*sic*]. [Doc was never an officer in Dodge City, and probably did not engage in the Dodge City War.]

The gathering of the gunfighters continued and Earp's arrival was announced by the *Ford County Globe* of June 5, 1883, with the following notation: "Wyatt Earp, a former marshal of Dodge City, arrived in the city from the west, last Thursday. Wyatt is looking well and glad to get back to his old haunts, where he is well and favorably known."

Attesting to the peaceable intent of the Short-Masterson Faction, if victory for Luke Short and Bat Masterson could be obtained by peaceful means, the *Globe* of June 12, 1883, said: "Within the past week the city had more distinguished visitors and more ex-city and county officers in it than ever saw together at any one time. It was a regular reunion of old-timers. They all appeared to have something to say about our late trouble and felt a deep interest in the future prosperity of our city." What the paper did not say was that the visitors were all armed and ready for war.

*An adaptation of a pen and
ink drawing of Wyatt Earp
from the 1896 San
Francisco EXAMINER.
(Turner Collection).*

Chapter 8

WYATT REFEREES

"Wyatt Earp Discusses His Decision in the Sharkey-Fitzsimmons Fight," was the heading for an interview published by the San Francisco EXAMINER in its Thursday morning, December 3, 1896, edition.

When I decided this contest in favor of Sharkey I did so because I believed Fitzsimmons deliberately fouled him, and under the rules the Sailor was entitled to the decision. I would have been willing to allow half-fouls——that is fouls that might be considered partly accidental to pass by with only a reprimand, but in such a case as this I could only do my duty.

Julian approached me before the contest and said he had heard stories to the effect that I favored Sharkey. We talked a few moments and he went away apparently satisfied that everything was on the square.

Any talk to the effect that I was influenced in any way to decide wrongly against Fitzsimmons is rubbish. I saw Sharkey but once before in my life and that was when he boxed with Corbet. I had no reason to favor him. If I was to have allowed my feelings to govern me, my decision would have been the other way.

I am a pretty close observer and under most conditions I think I am cool. I went into the ring as referee to give a square decision, and so far as my conscience speaks I have done so. It made no difference to me who won: the victor should be the best man. As I have already said, I met Sharkey only once before tonight and that was when he fought Corbett. Tonight I was standing in the enclosure near the ring when I met him again.

I have met Fitzsimmons several times, the first, I believe, being four or five years ago, when one of the best friends I have in the country and one of the truest supporters Fitzsimmons ever had, Bat Masterson, introduced us. I am sure that Bat

Masterson lost a great deal of money on this fight, but I have always been able to decide against my own money and my friends can stand the consequence of such a decision.

I feel that I did what was right and honorable and feeling so I care nothing for the opinion of anybody. I saw the foul blow struck as plainly as I see you, and that is all there is to the story. In the fourth or fifth round I warned Fitzsimmons that he was fouling in the wrestling. In every clinch the tall man would force himself down upon Sharkey, who was fighting low, and attempt to smash him.

Fitzsimmons replied that he was not fighting foul. I answered that I wanted no more of it and demanded that he quit it and be squaare. I told him that I would warn Sharkey as I had warned him and that I would do something more than reprimand if the foul fighting continued.

There is one thing I regret. I should have given Sharkey the fight earlier in the contest, the fourth round I think it was, Fitz landed a left-handed blow and returned with his elbow, cutting Sharkey's eyebrow open. The Sailor should have had the fight then.

The foul blow of the right was seen plainly by me. Fitz smashed with his right on Sharkey's shoulder and then with an uppercut with the left he struck the Sailor below the belt. Sharkey was leaning over and the blow knocked him down. It was clearly a foul and before the Sailor moved I mentioned that the fight was over. The first blow had been weak and I believe that the second was intended for an uppercut but it struck foul. No man until now has ever questioned my honor. I have been in many places and in peculiar situations, but no one ever said, until tonight that I was guilty of a dishonorable act. And I will repeat that I decided in all fairness and with a judgement that was as true as my eyesight. I saw the foul blow.

WYATT EARP

THE END

HISTORICAL NOTES AND EDITORIAL COMMENTS

The fight between Thomas Sharkey and Robert Fitzsimmons presented in Mechanics Pavilion, San Francisco, on the night of December 2, 1896, resulted in one of the most controversial incidents in Wyatt Earp's life. The question of contention being, was referee Earp "fixed" as Fitzsimmons and his backers claimed, or did Earp render an honest decision as Sharkey's backers maintain? Wyatt Earp, a veteran referee of more than thirty fights, started this endless debate when he awarded the decision to Sailor Tom Sharkey on an eighth round foul punch.

The National Athletic Club had made elaborate preparations for the event. They erected a twenty-four foot ring in the center of the pavilion, the largest building of its kind in San Francisco, and arranged seating for 20,000 spectators. A huge crowd, estimated to be 10,000 people, waited outside to follow the progress of the fight by the variable screaming of the spectators as the fortunes of battle swayed to-and-fro between the fighters.

The experts in the boxing world favored Fitzsimmons because of his experience and great boxing skill; while Sharkey was the popular choice because of his strength, and rough-and-ready tactics that came close to beating "Gentleman Jim" Corbett in an earlier fight. The odds shortly before fight time reached 20 to 9 favoring Fitzsimmons to win the $10,000 prize.

When the rival camps could not agree on a referee, Earp was chosen by the National Athletic Club to do the job. This arrangement seemed to satisfy both fighters, but at 10 p.m. when the principals and the referee entered the ring an argument broke out between the two managers, Martin Julian and Dan Lynch. The "debate" was carried on in front of the crowd, with Julian claiming that Earp had been "fixed" and would not give his man (Fitzsimmons) a square deal. The fighers sat in their seats quietly, ignoring the argument that was taking place.

By 11:37 p.m. the crowd grew weary and drowned out the debate with wild applause, stomping of the feet, and the cry, "Earp, Earp, Give us Earp!" Only then did the fight start.

Julian's charges were a surprise to everyone, since Wyatt Earp had enjoyed the reputation of being a "square sport" and Fitzsimmons had always "given up his choice of referee" in his previous fights.

The fighters then took off their bathrobes and advanced to the center of the ring for instructions from the referee. Starting another argument, Fitzsimmons demanded that Sharkey remove the bandages that were wrapped around his hands. The Sailor promptly refused, but this potential tirade was cut short when Earp stepped forward and instructed Sharkey to remove the bandages.

The fight by rounds that was published by the Los Angeles *Times* of December 3, 1896, showed that the fight was much closer than many of the spectators believed. The final round is given below:

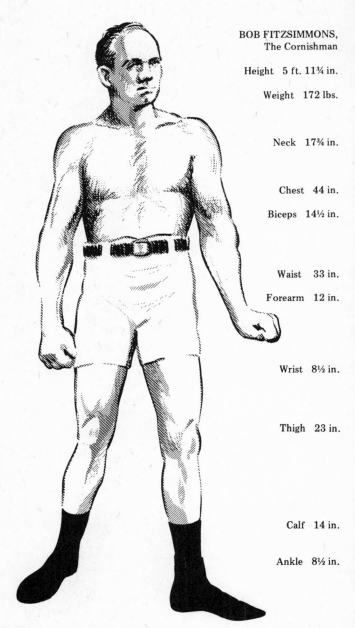

BOB FITZSIMMONS,
The Cornishman

Height 5 ft. 11¾ in.

Weight 172 lbs.

Neck 17¾ in.

Chest 44 in.

Biceps 14½ in.

Waist 33 in.

Forearm 12 in.

Wrist 8½ in.

Thigh 23 in.

Calf 14 in.

Ankle 8½ in.

The participants of the Fitsimmons-Sharkey fight that was refereed by Wyatt Earp in 1896. (Adapted from a drawing from the San Francisco EXAMINER, December 1, 1896.)

TOM SHARKEY,
The Sailor

Height   5 ft. 8¼ in.

Weight   172 lbs.

Neck   18 in.

Chest   45 in.

Biceps   15 in.

Waist   32 in.

Forearm   13½ in.

Wrist   7¾ in.

Thigh   22 in.

Calf   17¼ in.

Ankle   9 in.

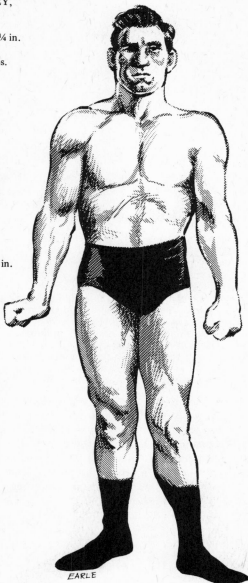

EARLE

*The Fitzsimmons-
Sharkey fight was
held in the Me-
chanics' Pavilion
in San Francisco,
December 2, 1896.*

ROUND EIGHT:
Fitzsimmons lead with his left for the face and missed, but a moment later landed a right swing on the head twice. Sharkey clinched and rushed Fitzsimmons to the ropes. Fitzsimmons tried a left on the head, and Tom countered with a right on the head. Fitzsimmons swung a right and left on the head. Sharkey landed a left swing on the head. Fitzsimmons swung a right on the head, and Sharkey came back with a left on the wind. Fitzsimmons jabbed Sharkey in the face with his left and swung a right on the jaw twice. He then landed his right-arm blow on the face. Sharkey went down. Sharkey out.

During a flurry of punches and counterpunches in the eighth round, Sharkey went down clutching his groin. Referee Wyatt Earp quickly stepped in and awarded the fight to the Sailor on a foul punch landed by Fitzsimmons on Sharkey's groin. He was obviously badly hurt and was carried from the ring (unconscious?) to his dressing room——followed by a doctor. Earp's decision was at first greeted with silence from the surprised crowd; but then, as they realized what had happened, hisses, curses, groans, and hoots, split the air. And in the background, remonstrating like madmen, Fitzsimmons and Julian were storming about the ring shouting to the spectators.

"Sharkey Describes That Decisive Blow," The San Francisco *Examiner*, December 3, 1896:

With the exception of an awful pain in my groin I cannot say that I feel any the worse for my encounter with Fitzsimmons. I did my best to put him to sleep and am satisfied that I had the best of it in every round.

Fitzsimmons pretends to be a very fair fighter and has a knack of making himself appear as such, before the public, but the truth of it is he uses the foulest tactics of any man I ever met.

His principal fouling is done with his elbow. He used his elbow on me dozens of times and in that way cut that deep gash over my left eye, which caused me to bleed so freely during the last four rounds.

Outside of that cut and the injury to my groin I am all right and am willing to meet him again at any time. I can whip him to a certainty and I believe he knows it himself.

At no time during the contest was I fatigued or in trouble until I received that foul blow. In fact I felt that I was getting stronger, as the fight progressed.

Fitzsimmons' blows did not hurt me——not one of them except that foul swing he made which laid me out.

While I was growing stronger and more confident of winning he was certainly losing in strength and quickness right along. This may not have impressed the spectators, but I could see it and I was taking advantage of his approaching collapse when he fouled me to save himself.

He has a trick of laughing and pretending that he is at ease, which deceived the crowd all through the fight.

Those punches I gave him around the ribs and abdomen distressed him. Had I not been quite so short in the reach I could have punched him out of the contest in about four rounds.

By keeping so far away from me he forced me to throw away many well-meant blows.

I am certain that Fitzsimmons fouled me deliberately. He did it to save himself from defeat.

It was getting too plain to him that I was gaining in strength while he was going downhill, so to speak, and rather than be knocked out he thought he would lose on a foul. Had he not delivered that nasty blow which crippled me I would certainly have finished him in that round——the eight, I believe it was.

I was for the moment paralyzed when I received that blow, and was wholly unable to protect myself. I felt myself sinking to the floor and I was doubled up in such a way that I could not guard myself from the fast uppercut which he sent in——I suppose as a finisher.

I am sorry that the question of supremacy was not settled on its merits rather than this way.

I can beat Fitzsimmons and I would far rather have knocked him out than win the purse on a foul. I don't think he will be anxious to meet me again, however, but if he does——well, I am open to all engagements. I am in the boxing business as a profession.

I intend to win the world's championship if the decision in this contest has not already given me the right to that title. I am not going to pose as a talking fighter either. If anybody wants to meet me they will always find me willing.

THOMAS J. SHARKEY.

"Fitzsimmons Accuses Earp of Fraud," The San Francisco *Examiner*, December 3, 1896.

I was simply robbed out of $10,000 by that decision, and what is more, I knew I was going to be robbed before I entered the ring.

W!.en I made that speech to the crowd telling them that I accepted Earp as a referee not withstanding the information that had been brought to me that he had been "fixed" to throw the fight to Sharkey, I knew I was a goner. But what else could I do? If I had refused to fight the whole country would have said that I was afraid to meet the man who nearly put Corbett out.

My reputation as a champion of the world was at stake and I could not afford to lose it for three times $10,000. The articles of agreement were that if Sharkey and I could not agree on a referee the club should have the selection of one. I suspected when Sharkey's people refused to agree to any of the men that I named that something was wrong, but I was not sure, so I told Julian to go on naming them until he got tired.

During all that time we couldn't get the other side to name anybody but a few unknown sporting men who couldn't get anybody to vouch for them. I didn't want to take anybody that didn't know anything about fighting, so we were left in a hole. Under the articles of agreement the naming of the referee went to the club and they picked Earp (who was a veteran referee).

The way I came to know that he had been fixed was this: In the lobby of the Baldwin Hotel today or, to be more exact, about 2 o'clock this afternoon, several men told Martin Julian not under any circumstances to accept Wyatt Earp, because he had agreed to throw the fight to Sharkey for a good sum of money. I am not at liberty to give the names of all the men who told that to Julian, but I can give you three of them, and they are men whose word will be accepted by sporting men all over the country. They are Riley Grannan, the racetrack plunger, Tom James, the man whom the house called to act as time-keeper tonight, and M. A. Gunset, one of the Police Commissioners of this town. They all told Julian that they knew Earp had been "fixed."

Major Frank McLaughlin also told me that I would be foolish to accept Earp, because he had heard that Earp had been "fixed." He didn't say he knew it, though, as the others did. That is the reason why both Julian and I held out so long against Earp at the ringside. But appearances were against us and with the whole house jeering at us we were left in a hole that we could not crawl out of any other way.

The final blow of the bout. (San Francisco EXAMINER, December 3, 1896).

Earp knows, and so does Sharkey, that I didn't hit the sailor where they said I did. My left landed straight in his stomach, where I had a right to hit him, and no other place. His lying down and groaning was all a part of the game. There was no reason for me to foul him, because I had him whipped anyway and could have finished him before the end of the round. It don't make any difference, though. As I telegraphed Dan Stuart to-night I am willing to meet both Sharkey and Corbett in the same ring any night Stuart wants to pull the fight off. I will say one thing for Corbett, and that is that I don't blame him for saying that he was robbed out of the Jackson fight in this town. No pugilist can get a square deal from the thieves who handle fighting in this city and it is a safe bet that the last big fight San Francisco will ever see was pulled off to-night. [Prize fighting was illegal anyway.]

"How Earp Was Chosen Referee." "James D. Gibbs of the National Club Tells Why that Selection Was Made." The San Francisco *Examiner*, Friday, December 4, 1896.

How did Wyatt Earp happen to be selected by the management of the National Athletic Club to referee the big contest between Sharkey and Fitzsimmons?

More than one person, in fact, asked that very question yesterday.

The question was answered by James D. Gibbs, the leading official of the club, last night. His answer was as follows:

"I want to say that if there was anything wrong about that match, or with the referee, or with anybody connected with it, I want the whole matter exposed. The club's reputation is at stake, and my personal reputation as well. I will say openly and publicly that I know nothing that would tend to show that the contest was not absolutely on the square.

"A week ago last Sunday I joined a party of gentlemen who had arranged a trip to San Francisco, their object being to visit Fitzsimmons at his training quarters. Wyatt Earp was a member of that party, but I did not know him. I had often heard of him, but had never seen him before. It was not until we were returning on the boat from San Salitor [?] however, that I made Earp's acquaintance. Billy Jorden, who served as master of ceremonies at the Pavilion introduced us. We all sat down and chatted about Fitzsimmons' condition, and about boxing contests in general. It was during this talk that Jordan said something about Mr. Earp having served as referee in many a good contest. In answer to a question asked by me, Mr. Earp acknowledged that he had refereed over thirty matches.

"Later on that day I told my associate, Mr. Groom, that I had discovered a man who would fill the bill in our big match in the event that Sharkey and Fitzsimmons failed to agree upon a referee. When I mentioned Earp's name he agreed with me that this was just the man. Nothing more was said about the matter for a week. We did not even tell Earp that we were thinking of asking him to serve. We did not know whether he would act or not. During this intervening week Mr. Groom prepared a list of eligible referees, but forgot to include Earp's name. This list was submitted to the respective managers of Sharkey and Fitzsimmons, after their first unsuccessful conference, and it was found that every man named had been rejected by them.

"Wyatt Earp's name was mentioned and I learned that he was regarded as a cool, courageous sport whose reputation for honesty had never been assailed.

"By this time it was practically settled that the managers of Sharkey and Fitzsimmons were not going to agree upon a referee so Groom and I had a consultation at the Baldwin Hotel. We concluded to ask Mr. Earp to serve. We took him into a private room in Police Commissioner Gunst's place and laid the matter before him. Earp at first refused. He said he was not seeking notoriety and would far rather be permitted to watch the contest from a spectator's seat. But by coaxing we finally got him to consent.

"Now, Mr. Julian, the manager of Fitzsimmons, and Mr. Lynch who looks out for Sharkey's interests both hailed this selection with expressions of satisfaction, and everybody we told about it said a better choice could not have been made. When the evening papers announced on the afternoon of the contest that Earp would be the referee, we received congratulations from all sides.

"It was not until I went to Fitzsimmons' dressing room that night to tell him to prepare to go into the ring that I heard of any objection to Earp. Julian and Fitzsimmons both said they had heard that he had been "fixed." I was thunderstruck. Well to make a long story short, they went into the ring and that long wrangle, with which everybody is familiar, took place. While they were talking Earp came to me and begged to be allowed to retire. But by this time I had become somewhat

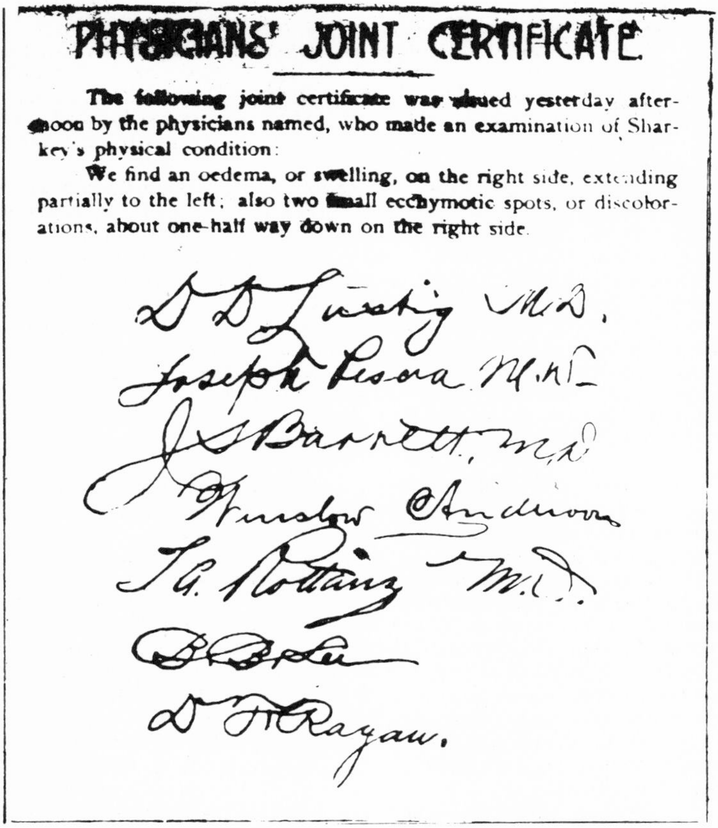

PHYSICIANS' JOINT CERTIFICATE

The following joint certificate was issued yesterday afternoon by the physicians named, who made an examination of Sharkey's physical condition:

We find an oedema, or swelling, on the right side, extending partially to the left; also two small ecchymotic spots, or discolorations, about one-half way down on the right side.

[handwritten signatures]

D. D. Lustig, M.D.
Joseph Pesara, M.D.
J. S. Barrett, M.D.
Winslow Anderson
J. G. Rotting, M.D.
[signature]
D. T. Ragan.

The Physician's Joint Certificate that stated that Sharkey had been fouled. (San Francisco EXAMINER, December 4, 1896).

worked up over the actions of Julian and Fitsimmons——believing as I did that they were not sincere——and I made Earp promise to stand his ground. Under the articles of agreement the club had the privilege to select the referee in the event that the principals could not agree upon a suitable man and at that late stage of the proceedings I proposed to stand by our selection. The spectators were becoming impatient and the delay was irritating.

"This is the entire story of how Wyatt Earp happened to be selected as referee, and I hope it will dispel any idea that there has been any collusion or jobbery.

"Like Sand on the Seashore: Innumerable Opinions of Those Who Discuss the Fitzsimmons-Sharkey Contest." The San Francisco *Examiner*, December 4, 1896.

Everybody that was present at the fight seems to have had an opinion of his own in regard to the blow which is said to have put Sharkey to sleep. Many claimed that Referee Earp rendered a just decision and that Fitzsimmons delivered a foul blow. Many others, on the other hand, claim that Fitzsimmons did not deliver a foul blow and that the decision of the referee was unjust. The following are a few of the many conflicting opinions of men who, while they do not claim to be experts, are qualified to give an opinion in regard to what they saw:

W. H. C. Fowler, Insurance Manager: "I think it was a foul blow and I judge it from the fact that Sharkey was doubled up, fell and was carried helpless from the ring. It must have been a terrible blow. The fight was so rapid that I cannot say I saw the blow delivered. It was all done in the twinkling of an eye.

William E. Dargie: "Fitzsimmons had the best of the battle all the way through. I was looking at the right when the knock-out blow was landed, and I did not see any sign of a foul blow. The decision of the referee was raw.

George F. Hatton: "It was a funny thing that the forty, or more reporters who were watching the fight could not see any foul blow. I was in the press stand seated next to the Eastern reporter, who used his glasses. In my opinion Fitzsimmons had the best of it and should have had the decision.

Charles Gardiner, clerk to Oakland's Chief of Police: "The decision of the referee was fair and square. I saw the foul blow delivered by Fitzsimmons just as plainly as possible. It was clearly a foul blow and I called the attention of a friend to the fact at the time. Sharkey had the best of the fight and he was entitled to the decision just as it was given. It was the only thing that Earp could do and be square.

James Landregan: "Earp's decision was all right. Fitzsimmons hit Sharkey a foul blow, below the belt, and the Sailor was given the fight on a foul, as all of the rules of the ring demand. There was no doubt about it, Sharkey was struck in a vital spot. All his actions after that uppercut landed showed that he was injured in a way that could be accounted for only by a foul. He put up a good fight and there might have been a different ending but for the foul blow. The referee knew what he was about when he gave the fight to the Sailor.

Celia Ann Blaylock, Wyatt Earp's second wife who committed suicide in 1888 in Pinal, Arizona. (Glenn G. Boyer Collection).

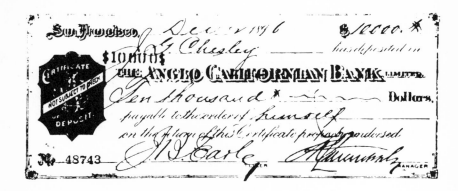

A reproduction of the $10,000 purse signed by J. B. Earle. (San Francisco EXAMINER).

There were numerous other persons who gave their opinions to this newspaper reporter concerning the fight and the referee's decision. Usually they were almost equally divided between Sharkey and Fitzsimmons. It would be an interesting study, although impossible to conduct at this late date, to establish the correlation, if any, between a person's betting choice, and the referee's decision in this fight. An old and valid axiom, "money talks," would seem to apply in this case.

"Decide to Pay the Check. Relying on the Joint Certificate of Six Physicians the National Club Will Not Delay Payment of the Purse." San Francisco *Examiner*, December 4, 1896.

We withheld the payment of the check ($10,000) because of the dissatisfaction on the part of many of the audience. Some of them claimed that the referee was a party to a job to cheat Fitzsimmons. In order that Fitzsimmons and his backers might have every opportunity to institute the legal proceedings they threatened after the contest, we, as directors of the National Athletic Club requested the Anglo-California Bank to withhold payment on the check for the time being, to avoid any possible future charge on the part of Julian or Fitzsimmons that the money was paid over before they had an opportunity to prepare their pleadings. If a foul blow had been dealt by Fitzsimmons, we knew that an examination by physicians would prove it. Being unable to secure a satisfactory examination Wednesday night, we furthermore thought it advisable to withhold payment of the check until we were satisfied that the condition of Sharkey gave corroborative evidence of what his seconds claimed. An examination was made today by six physicians, and we, on their certificate, decided we had no right to further delay payment of the check.

J. J. Groom,
J. D. Gibbs.

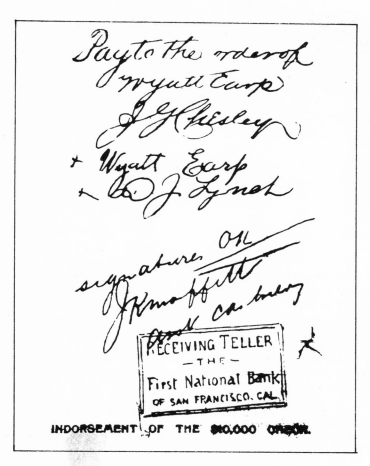

The endorsement on the back side of the check shows Wyatt Earp's signature above that of D. J. Lynch. (San Francisco EXAMINER).

Wyatt Earp's Northern Saloon in Tonopah, Nevada, in 1902. The people are unidentified. (Nevada Historical Society).

"What They Say in 'Frisco." From the Los Angeles *Times*, December 4, 1896:

The city is divided as to the result of the Fitzsimmons-Sharkey fight, which continues to be the topic of the hour. No one questions that Fitzsimmons had the fight practically won in the eight round, and many assert that he was unjustly deprived of the decision. Sharkey's friends vehemently assert that he was knocked out by a foul blow and was consequently under the rules entitled to the honors of victory, including the purse of $10,000.

A third class base their opinions solely upon the report of the physicians in attendance upon Sharkey. The doctors point to the swollen and discolored condition of the Sailor's skin in the region of the groin as evidence of a foul blow, and some ardent Fitzsimmons advocates reply that this condition was purposely caused by an injection of a drug immediately after the fight. A number of physicians and newspaper men were present in Sharkey's room this afternoon when an examination of his injuries were made. All were convinced that Sharkey's condition was the result of a foul blow.

Many prominent men, however, condemn the decision and refuse to believe that there was any fouling. Such men as Police Commissioner Gunst, Riley Grannan, Major Frank McLaughlin, who. was chairman of the Republican State Central Committee, and others believe that Fitzsimmons should have received the decision.

It is pointed out that the whole affair has a disagreeable look. The facts are cited that Lynch, Sharkey's backer, refused to consider the name of anyone as referee, declined every name suggested by Julian and refused to suggest any man himself, leaving the selection with the few individuals comprising the National Club. As soon as the club announced its choice of Wyatt Earp, famous as a horseman and a bad man from Arizona, but not as a ring expert, the odds, which had been 10 to 4 against Sharkey, unaccountably rose to 10 to 6, with more Sharkey money offered than could be well handled.

It is recounted that there were whispers yesterday afternoon that Sharkey would be favored in the decision, and these rumors reaching Fitzsimmons' ears, he requested the club to substitute anyone else as referee. Even at ringside, when both Julian and Fitzsimmons stated in Earp's presence that they had been told he intended to referee unfairly, Earp stood quietly by and insisted on acting as referee despite the protest.

It is pointed out that Fitzsimmons fought a clean, skillful, scientific, and winning battle, while Sharkey was rough and unfair, with many fouling tactics, such as clasping Fitzsimmons around the legs below the knee and attempting to throw him. For these offences it is charged that Sharkey was not even reproved by the referee. It is claimed that the uppercut on Sharkey's chin in the eight round was really a knock-out blow, and that no foul blow was delivered by Fitzsimmons, but that Sharkey, when knocked out alleged the foul blow as an excuse, although if the latter allegation be true, then Sharkey is a more clever actor than many have supposed. *All this constitutes the case of Fitzsimmons, by which his attorney expects to prove the existence of a conspiracy to deprive Fitzsimmons of the purse of $10,000.*

DIDN'T LIKE EARP

Martin Julian, Fitzsimmons' manager, has made a statement to the Associated Press in which he says:

". . . Early in the day when we met to select a referee, Lynch would not agree to any of the men whose names I mentioned. I then asked him to name a man and he declined saying he preferred to leave it to the National Club. The Club officials selected Earp, and although I knew nothing about the man, I thought he must be allright. When I was told that Earp was crooked I took Fitzsimmons to the pavilion at 7, instead of 9 o'clock as I first intended. I saw Groom and Gibbs and told them plainly that Fitzsimmons would not go into the ring if Earp was to be referee, and I told them why. I offered to take any other man in town except Earp, and thought there was plenty of time to make a selection, nothing was done.

"Finally, when the big fight was called, I made the announcement from the ring, charging Earp had been fixed. The big crowd was impatient of delay and hissed and hooted me. I saw that it would not do to take Bob from the ring. If I had the crowd would have mobbed us. We finally decided to go ahead and do the best we could in spite of the referee. It was owing to Bob's distrust of Earp that he fought so fairly and so cautiously. He knew that he must take no chances and he did not. When Earp saw that Sharkey was gone, he called the foul and Sharkey pretended to be hurt. It was a prearranged scheme."

THE AUSTRALIAN SUES

Late this afternoon Bob Fitzsimmons, through his attorney, commenced suit in the Superior Court to restrain the Anglo-California Bank from paying the $10,000 purse awarded the Sailor by referee Earp. Fitzsimmons charges conspiracy between Sharkey, the National Athletic Club, and others whose names are not given, to award the purse to Sharkey under any circumstances.

Fitzsimmons alleges that before Earp was selected as referee this arrangement was made, and that had he known about it he would have refused to enter the ring. He therefore prays, as he "discomfited" Sharkey, so that the latter was unable to proceed, and on account of the alleged conspiracy that the Anglo-California Bank, Tom Sharkey, David Lynch, John Doe, and Richard Roe, be enjoined from collecting the money on the certificate of deposit, and that the court award said certificate to Fitzsimmons.

Judge Sanderson granted the injunction prayed for, and the case will soon be tried in court. The National Club is composed of J. J. Groom and John Gibbs, local men.

WYATT EARP ARRESTED

When Wyatt Earp appeared in the ring last night to act as referee, he was disarmed by Police Captain Whittman, who took from the Arizona man a large-sized pistol. Tonight Earp was arrested on a charge of carrying concealed weapons. He was released on $10 bail.

Another item from the Los Angeles *Times*, December 5, 1896.

WYATT EARP SAYS HE IS SORRY HE DIDN'T QUIT

. . . Bets on the fight are being paid off today. Some pool-sellers settled yesterday, and the remaining poolrooms are paying Sharkey's backers today. One bookmaker paid out $25,000 this afternoon to holders of Sharkey tickets.

Referee Wyatt Earp, who was arrested last night charged with carrying a concealed weapon, was in police court today. Earp asked and obtained a continuance till Tuesday.

PHILOSOPHICAL REFLECTIONS

Wyatt Earp, the most-talked-of-man of the hour, takes a philosophical view of the criticisms that are being heaped upon him for the decision of Wednesday night, and says that he will wait for time to set him right with the public.

"If I had any fears that I erred in my decision they would have disappeared when I saw Sharkey today." he said last night. "Sharkey did not strike a foul blow to my mind. At the break he struck Fitzsimmons as soon as his arm was free, but that is following Queensbury rules. It is true that it was agreed that there was to be no fighting at the break, but my instructions from the club were not to be technical, but to give the audience a good fight for their money.

"I have one regret about the whole matter, and that is that I did not leave the ring when Julian objected to me. I thought of doing it, but it occurred to me that it would be quitting under fire, and I made up my mind to stay until ordered off by the club. I am sorry that I acted as referee at all.

The only inconvenience Fitzsimmons is suffering as a result of his meeting with the sailor is a painful swelling of the joints of the hands.

"I have nothing more to say in explanation," he said, "except what we surmised yesterday, and that is that members of the National Club, were in this deal with Lynch and Sharkey to job us, and what is more, we are going to prove it in court.

"Had it not been [Fitzsimmons speaking] that I was saving my hands as much as possible I would have put Sharkey out in the second round. His head is as hard as a bullet, and I must have landed on him there fully forty times. With my coming fight with Corbett in view I didn't think it worth while to punch my hands out of shape. In a rough-and-tumble scrap Sharkey might do a man some damage, as he is stocky and strong, but in a boxing contest or in a ring battle no sane man would ever bet a dollar on him if there was a referee present who knew his business."

Police Commissioner Gunst is satisfied that the fight was "jobbed," so that he has announced that there will be no more prizefighting. [He and his 'police broke the law in allowing the illegal Sharkey-Fitzsimmons fight to take place] in San Francisco if his influence can prevent it.

The mystery of Sharkey's injury has not yet been satisfactorily solved, and to an operation for the purpose of manufacturing the evidence necessary to back up the claim of foul. Certain it is that when Sharkey was taken to his room at the Windsor Hotel, no one was allowed to speak to him until "Dr." Lee had worked on him. When "Dr." Lee commenced his examination of Sharkey the portieres were closely drawn across the bedroom door and pinned so that no one could see in. A few minutes later, after some low talk was heard, Sharkey began to groan as if in pain. Many believe that the "injury" Sharkey received was given him at this time.

A WORD FOR EARP.

In 1875, Wyatt Earp, the referee of the Fitzsimmons-Sharkey fight, was a policeman in Wichita [Kansas] under the notorious Chief of Police, Mike Meager.

Dick Cogell, who succeeded Meager as chief says, "Earp is a man who never smiled or laughed. He was the most fearless man I ever saw. He was Marshal at Ellsworth [Dodge City], Kansas, when that was a cattle shipping point, and he was a success. He is an honest man.

All officers here who were associated with him declare that he is honest, and would have decided according to his belief in the face of an arsenal.

From the Los Angeles *Times*, December 10, 1896:
"Sensational Stories About Earp and the Sailor."

The legal contest between Sharkey and Fitzsimmons for the possession of the $10,000 purse has commenced before the Superior Court. The excitement was intense when the proceedings began in the crowded courtroom, and Manager Julian brought out his witnesses to prove the conspiracy which he stated had deprived Fitzsimmons of the purse.

"Australian Billy" Smith, one of Sharkey's trainers, was the first witness. He detailed his work in connection with preparing Sharkey for the ring, and said that when the question of selecting a referee was mooted in Sharkey's training quarters, he was asked to suggest a referee. The witness suggested Hiram Cook, and Lynch then asked him if he knew Cook well enough to "talk business with him." Afterward the witness said, Lynch characterized Cook as "no good," because he would not favor his own brother in a fight.

On the evening of the fight Sharkey told witnesses that Earp had been fixed as referee, and that "Earp was all right." The witness des-

Wyatt lived here at 1003 Golden Gate Avenue, San Francisco, when he was interviewed by the press in 1896. Wyatt and Josephine occupied the top floor. The building was purchased in 1968 by the Federal Redevelopment Agency for demolishment. (Jack Smoot Collection).

The floor plan of Wyatt's apartment. (Opposite page).

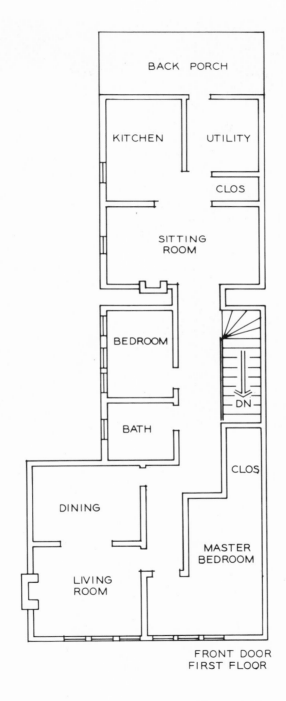

Wyatt Earp lived here during his mining days in Earp, California. (Turner Collection).

cribed the uproar over the preliminaries to the fight, and said that when Fitzsimmons objected to the bandages on Sharkey's wrists, Earp went over to Sharkey's corner and said: "Take off those cloths. It will be all right anyway."

The witness said that when Sharkey received the knockout blow on the jaw in the eight round, Lynch said to Sharkey: "Lie low. Hold your hands on your groin, and pretend to faint with pain." Sharkey was then carried to a room. He did not appear to be much hurt. The witness said Allen, another trainer, "Removed Sharkey's bandages and did the work which caused the swelling." Sharkey was then driven to his hotel in a hack. Allen was with him. Sharkey was all right.

George Allen, another of Sharkey's trainers, corroborated the story of the previous witnesses, adding that several physicians were refused admittance when Sharkey was undergoing the operation with Allen, which produced the evidence of a foul. Lynch said that no doctor should come into the room and interfere with his plans.

The witness said Sharkey told him the National Athletic Club was composed of Groom, Gibbs, Lynch, and Sharkey, and that Sharkey was to receive 20 per cent of the proceeds of the fight after the purse was deducted. Sharkey said his three partners in the National Club were broke and Sharkey had had to advance $2,500 for preliminary expenses which left the sailor pugilist stranded financially.

The witness said that a few days before the fight Sharkey told him he thought Earp would be the right kind of a referee for him, and added it would be worth $2,500 to Earp if he were the "right" kind of a referee.

Smith was cross-examined by Sharkey's counsel, but nothing of any importance was elicited. The case then went over until tomorrow.

Trainer Allen, who has not yet appeared as a witness, will then go on the stand and corroborate Smith's testimony.

"Australian" Billy Smith, one of Sharkey's trainers said today: "I talked to Sharkey at 10 o'clock on the morning of the fight. He told me that Earp would be chosen referee and that the game was for him to be given the decision on a foul in the first round, or as soon after that as Fitzsimmons hit him a body blow of any kind. Then Needham would be crazy if they found out he had told me. When the men got into the ring, and Fitzsimmons objected to Sharkey's hand bandages, Earp came over to our corner and whispered to Sharkey: "Take off the bandages, Tom; it will be all right, anyhow."

"Well things went on until the eight round, and saw Sharkey fall. I did not see the blow that sent him down. I climbed up into the ring, picked him up and hauled him to his corner. In a minute or two Lynch came up into the ring and rushing over to Sharkey, said to him: 'Now keep your hands down and pretend to be in great pain,' but Sharkey was so badly dazed by the blow on the head that he forgot to do what Lynch ordered, except once in a while. Lynch then told us to take him to the room. We did so, and then laid him on a cot and closed all the doors. Lynch said: 'Don't ___ ___ soul in ___ reporters, doctors, or any-body else.'

"On visiting Sharkey the night after the fight the latter called me to his pillow. He said: 'What kind of a fight did I put up?' I said: 'Pretty good.' He said: 'That ___ _ _ ____ can beat Corbett in two rounds. He hits like the hind foot of a mule.' I told Sharkey he would have a 'cauliflower' ear for sure and he said, 'Yes, ___ it; it will spoil my good looks.' "

ATTACHED BY CREDITORS

A remarkable thing about the tangle consequent upon the decision of the referee in the Fitzsimmons-Sharkey fiasco is that all the men who figure as principals in the affair, outside of Sharkey, have been attached for various sums by wrathy creditors. And now the sailor himself is to be dragged into the net, for two attachment suits against him are being prepared, the creditors being two old trainers, who claim in all $1,100 for their services.

The present combination of circumstances will probably lead in the near future to the National Sporting Club hanging up a purse of $20,000 for a second fight between Sharkey and Fitzsimmons.

J. J. Rauer, the collector, has brought about the state of affairs that has led to the probability of the latter proposition. He is now forcing attachment suits against Earp, Fitzsimmons, and Lynch and today will begin another legal process of the same nature against Sharkey. Among these four men undoubtedly rests the rightful ownership of the $10,000 check. If Rauer gets judgement against all of them——and he confidently expects to——the check will be tied up indefinitely and the money it represents will virtually revert to the club. In that event and in order to clear the organization of the imputation of unfair dealing lately cast on it, Groom and Gibbs intend to offer the men another battle and will double the purse.

Fitzsimmons will jump at the chance if it is offered, but says that Sharkey will never fight now that there is no chance of his fixing the referee a second time. Sharkey will not express any opinion one way or the other, but referred his questioners to Danny Lynch. The latter was not accessible last night . . .

From the Los Angeles *Daily Times* of December 18, 1896:

SHARKEY WINS AGAIN

The fight between Sharkey and Fitzsimmons for the possession of the $10,000 purse was concluded today when Judge Sanderson of the Superior Court dissolved the injunction restraining the Anglo-California Bank from cashing the check.

The counsel for Sharkey called the attention of the court to the State law forbidding prize fighting between which and "a glove contest," he maintained, there was no difference, and he therefore argued that a case involving the possession of a purse for prize fighting had no standing in court. The judge concurred in this view, and said he would have terminated the proceedings earlier had that point been called to his judicial attention. The court held that under California Statute the civic Board of Supervisors had no more power to legalize a prize fight than to sanction a duel. The decision concluded as follows:

"There is no question in my mind that the parties in this engagement, exhibition, or whatever you call it——the complaint calls it a boxing contest——are indictable under the law, and that the people who witnessed it are amenable as law-breakers. I understand that these exhibitions are given: and they are given because the people and the police wink at them. But no court will recognize any such proceeding, and there is no doubt in my mind that this injunction should be dissolved, and it would have been dissolved if the motion had been made immediately upon the heels of issuing it, as the court in part expected.

"The order to dissolve the injunction will be granted, and the complaint be stricken from the files."

The whole proceedings were over.

The ending of the court battle between Fitzsimmons and Sharkey, for the possession of the $10,000 purse, was as unsatisfactory as the decision of the referee that followed the fight. In each case the contest was not allowed to proceed to a satisfactory finish.

After hearing two days of testimony [Fitzsimmons' side], the Magistrate threw the suit out of court. The fight itself, he pointed out, was illegal and all of the participants, including the spectators, were subject to arrest. "The Board of Supervisors," the judge counseled, "had no more power to legalize a prize fight than to sanction a duel." Even the police were lawbreakers when they allowed the prize fight to take place in San Francisco. The judge promptly dissolved the injunction, which had stopped payment on the check and the proceedings came to an abrupt halt.

Right or wrong, Referee Wyatt Earp's decision had stood up. Sharkey remained the winner in both the ring and the courts. Fitzsimmons protested vehemently, but there was nothing he could do but accept each decision: from the referee and the court.

The court's withdrawal from the case, due to lack of jurisdiction, settled the ownership of the $10,000 purse. Still, there remained many questions left unanswered:

1. Did Earp throw the fight to Sharkey by calling a fake foul?

2. Did Fitzsimmons foul Sharkey, either deliberately or accidentally?

3. Could a foul have been determined immediately after the fight by a medical examination of Sharkey?

4. Could evidence of a foul have been produced by Sharkey's trainers after the fight?

The best account of the Sharkey-Fitzsimmons fight, written by an eyewitness at ringside, was Edward H. Hamilton's, "Yes, It Was a Great

Fight, But . . . " Hamilton's story covered the fight from every angle. It was published in the December 3, 1896, issue of the San Francisco *Examiner*. However, the unanswered questions will remain unanswerable for many. Only the known evidence can be presented.

New information has come to light on the Sharkey-Fitzsimmons fight from Tom Sharkey himself. It is in the form of a letter to Glenn G. Boyer dated October 26, 1965, from Roy Earp, formerly an Inspector on the Oakland, California, police force. His letter is printed with Mr. Boyer's permission:

26 Oct. 65
Oakland, Calif.

Mr. Glenn G. Boyer:
Sir:
Thank you for the two pictures also for your interest in my Father and Cousin Wyatt.

Regret that I cannot help you on the cause and result of the fight staged in Lamar, Missouri.

My Mother and Father were divorced so many years ago that I can no longer remember in sensible detail any of the many stories he used to tell me about Wyatt Earp's actions.

One story I do recall fairly well was one told to me by Sailor Tom Sharkey in 1925 in Oakland.

Sharkey was an old time former heavyweight pugilist great, who had fought the champions and near champions. He was on a vaudeville tour in 1925 on the Orpheum circuit and he promised Wyatt he would look me up when they——Sharkey and former Champion Jim Jefferies—played Oakland in a 3 round, one minute per round, boxing exhibition.

Sharkey looked me up and I spent five days with him driving him around in between shows.

I could tell by the way Sharkey talked that he was a firm friend of Wyatts. He also seemed to hold Wyatt in awe. He said there was something mysterious——he said "spooky"——about the way Wyatt looked at an enemy.

After the prize fight between Sharkey and Champion Bob Fitzsimmons, which Wyatt refereed and tried to give to Sailor Tom on a foul, there developed some animosity on Fitzsimmons side toward Wyatt.

Incidentally Sharkey swore to me the Champion struck him several foul blows in the groin.

Sharkey naming places, dates and times, which I have since forgotten, said a few days after the fight Fitzsimmons was telling a group of approximately 30 men in a saloon at a long bar, about how Earp had tried to rob him of his title and that if he ever met Wyatt Earp face to face and within punching distance, he would show everyone that he would knock Wyatt cold.

Sharkey said Wyatt was aware of the talk Fitz had been making since the fight but hadn't said anything about it.

Sharkey said it was about the middle of the day (afternoon) when he and Wyatt entered the saloon and heard the tail end of Fitz's remarks. Wyatt told Tom, stay out of this, and walked toward Fitz at the bar.

Wyatt and Josephine are buried in The Hills of Eternity Memorial Park in Colma near San Francisco. (William Oster Collection)

The room got very quiet and the hangersons hastily backed away.

Fitz suddenly became aware of Wyatt standing shoulder to shoulder with him. Wyatt ordered a shot of whiskey and holding the small shot glass in his left hand raised it to his lips but did not drink it then.

His right hand was just a few inches from the butt of his six gun, which was under his waist band belt, with just the handle showing. Then Wyatt slowly turned toward Fitz and looked him in the eye and they were only about two feet apart.

Sharkey said Fitz stumbled back a few steps as if he had been struck, then turned and hastily walked out of the saloon.

Then Wyatt drunk his drink, waited a few minutes looking at the crowd, then he left the bar with Sharkey.

Sharkey said later inquiries showed that Fitz had hurried to his Hotel two blocks away, grabbed an extra shirt and sox, and asked the Hotel owner to hide him until the next stage left town, then forward his suitcase and other belongings to a destination Fitz gave him.

Sharkey said not a word was spoken between the two men in the saloon.

Please excuse me if I have rambled on like this, but your letter brought back old memories of 40 years ago when Sharkey brought me a message from Wyatt Earp to please come visit him in the Long Beach-Los Angeles area and he would get me a good steady job there if I wanted to stay.

I told Sharkey I would visit Wyatt soon, but other things came along and it was not to be.

Good wishes in your reasearch.

Sincerely — Roy M. Earp.

THE
EARLY WEST

Index

THE
EARLY WEST

Alford E. Turner

Alford E. Turner, a retired public school teacher, is a collector, writer, and researcher, having devoted twenty-five years following in the foosteps of the Earp family. During this time, Mr. Turner has compiled one of the largest collections of information and Earpiana.

He was born on a farm outside Haddam, Kansas, on October 25, 1912. At the age of seven, he moved with his family to Peoria, Arizona, where he completed grade school and high school. He graduated with a Bachelor of Arts degree from Arizona State University in 1939, and a Master of Arts degree in 1950.

Al Turner became interested in Earp history when he read Stuart N. Lake's book, *Wyatt Earp: Frontier Marshal*, in 1955. He soon learned that history books were often unreliable or incomplete which prompted him to seek primary research in order to learn more of the true facts surrounding the lives of the Earps.

Throughout the years he has compiled a body of factual information by researching old newspapers, deeds, bills of sale, court records, coroner's records, mining records, probate records, marriage records, birth records, death records, great registers, census reports, Civil War records, and personal records.

For the past six years, Mr. Turner has lived in Tombstone, Arizona, with is wife Margie, where he is researching the records in the Cochise County Courthouse in an attempt to locate the data for a definitive history of the Earp family.

Al Turner is recognized as one of the outstanding scholars on the history of the Earps. His research is based on primary sources that he has visited and studied firsthand.

JIM
EARLE
NOV 73